MORE FOR ALL THE FAMILY

Also by Michael Botting:

For All the Family
Teaching the Families
Family Worship
Reaching the Families
Twenty Questions on Baptism

More for All the Family

Edited by

MICHAEL BOTTING

CPAS

KINGSWAY PUBLICATIONS
EASTBOURNE

Front cover illustration by Graeme Skinner

British Library Cataloguing in Publication Data

Botting, Michael
More for all the family.
1. Christian church. Sermons
I. Title
251.02

ISBN 0-86065-861-9 Kingsway
907750-57-5 CPAS

The Church Pastoral Aid Society (CPAS) is an Evangelical
Anglican organisation set up to support and help local
parishes in their work of mission. CPAS provides materials
and training for leaders of all age groups in the church
family, including clergy, housegroup leaders and those
involved in children's and youth work.
CPAS: Athena Drive, Tachbrook Park, Warwick CV34 6NG.

Printed in Great Britain for
KINGSWAY PUBLICATIONS LTD
1 St Anne's Road, Eastbourne, E Sussex BN21 3UN by
Courier International Ltd, Tiptree, Essex
Typeset by Nuprint Ltd, Harpenden, Herts.

This book is dedicated to Mary, my wife, the most constructive critic of all my family-service talks; to my daughter, Ruth, and son, David, who are active members of their own churches, despite their father's talks; and to my grandchildren, Daniel, Matthew, James and Emma, who I pray may come to know the Lord Jesus, perhaps through the ministry of family services.

Contents

Foreword

The name of Michael Botting has become almost synonymous with family services! He has led and inspired the enormous developments in these services countrywide—services which are often the growth-point of the church.

Since his last book on this theme, he has moved from a large city-centre church to two small country churches (and to being one of the two pioneers of a very successful lay training scheme in the Chester Diocese). His readiness to adapt, think and rethink in a different situation has made his family-service work even more on target for *all* sorts of parishes.

Here we have a marvellous collection of material—giving preparation and presentation in detail. The illustrations and visuals are not allowed to be 'the thing', but are always servants to the word. They are not mere entertainment, but effective communication (how much adults will learn too!).

I commend this book enthusiastically. I hope it will be used widely and effectively, for good preparation and presentation leads to good propagation of the vibrant truth of God.

+ MICHAEL CESTR

Introduction

The only excuse I can offer for editing another volume of family-service talks is that hardly a week passes when I get asked when another is coming. A further indication of the need is that the previous volume *For All The Family* (Kingsway/Falcon, 1984) has recently had its fourth printing.

Recent publications relating to family services

These talks are obviously primarily designed to be used in family services, and since my previous book was published, several important books have appeared that relate in some way to this type of service. For example, Josephine Bax in *The Good Wine* (Church House Publishing [CHP], 1986) cites family services as being the big growth-point in many parishes, and particularly commends the Church Pastoral Aid Society (CPAS) service as excellent. That same year *Church Family Worship* (Hodder & Stoughton) was published, edited by Michael Perry. The themes suggested in that book have guided me in the selection of subjects for this book, but my original idea to keep to the same order proved too complicated, so I have adopted the same sections as in my previous books.

In 1988 *Children in the Way* (NS/CHP) was published, being a Report from the General Synod Board of Education, in which an attempt is made to find a suitable model for the church's task in Christian education in the life of the Anglican parish. The benefits of the 'school' model are acknowledged, but as a contemporary model, is thought to have limitations. The 'family' model is then considered and accepted as in many ways being an enriching addition to the Anglican vocabulary. However, the much preferred model is that of the 'pilgrim church'. I must leave readers to draw their own conclusions, but would like to make a plea not to reject the 'family' model too hastily.

Jesus developed the concept of God as Father when teaching his disciples about prayer. He spoke of them as children of God and as entering into this relationship by spiritual birth. The apostle Paul encouraged disciples to think of God in the most intimate of fatherly terms with the use of 'Abba', the equivalent of our term 'daddy'. Writing to the Ephesians, he said, 'I kneel before the Father, from whom his whole family in heaven and on earth derives its name' (Eph 3:14–15). The same thought is not far removed from other metaphors, such as the church being a 'household' (Gal 6:10 RSV) and Jesus several times in his parables refers to God as being a 'householder' (Mt 13:27, 21:33 RSV). Now *Children in the Way* quotes Dr Gloria Durka of Fordham University, who defines the family as 'any small group of people who consider themselves bound to each other by enduring ties, and who are responsible for each other's wellbeing.' [1] If we accept that as a secular definition of family, then surely the church should be able to say the same, only writ large, because the head of the Christian family is none other than God the Father himself; Christ is 'making his home' in the individual hearts of genuine members through faith (Eph 3:17 GNB), and we have the uniting and strengthening power of the Holy Spirit available to us, to enable us to act responsibly to fellow members for mutual wellbeing.

The last book I must mention that is of particular significance here is *Patterns for Worship* (CHP, 1989), being a Report by the Liturgical Commission of the General Synod of the Church of England. As early as page 2, under the heading of 'family services', it helpfully lists some of the criticisms voiced against such services. I summarise: childish; banal; too free to be identifiably Anglican; too focused on the nuclear family to the exclusion of the single, bereaved, divorced and elderly; no 'bridge' to more mature worship and often too dominated by the whim of the leader, with little or no consultation with the PCC.

I am only too aware from personal experience that such descriptions can be an accurate diagnosis; indeed, they have been aired in articles and correspondence in the church press. Mercifully, the Report goes on to state that in other places the family service '...is the main sign of hope for the church, reflecting an enormous amount of creative energy and the kind of God-centred worship that is resulting in a considerable growth of new Christians.' [2] The Report then lists, first, positive answers to the above criticisms, and then attempts to define what is meant by 'family', for whom the family service caters, giving it the very widest interpretation, so that no one in the parish could feel excluded. This Report is not enthusiastic about the title 'family service' and welcomes the concept of the 'pilgrim church' model promoted in *Children in the Way* as providing some exciting educational possibilities, but doubts if 'pilgrim service' would convey the required image.

Patterns for Worship should most certainly become a resource on the shelf of every leader of Anglican worship, and not least of those responsible for leading 'family services'—or whatever they may eventually be called.

The changing face of families and family services

When this book was first conceived, I sought help from a friend of long standing, Margaret Old of Scripture Union, who has had extensive experience of family worship and education over the years, especially with all-age learning. She had written to me about the considerable change in family life over the past two decades, and how this has had to be reflected in the change in the family service in her own local church. Her comments are so valuable that I quote them at length.

Figures for the UK in 1989 showed that only 28% of households consisted of a married couple with children, a percentage almost equalled by households consisting of a single person. There are children, too, who are in permanent transit between households. The family service today has to demonstrate that the local church is meant to be the Christian's large, extended family, the kind of family which the West lost with the coming of the industrial revolution and which was fragmented further as we became a highly mobile society.

During our church worship I have seen a four-year-old move happily from her mother to another adult several rows behind, and then to yet another. She feels at home. She knows she is part of one family. We worship as one family rather than as a collection of family units. The service still forms a bridge into our church's life, but it is not only a bridge. It cannot be mainly for fringe-people and yet be a true family at the same time. Yet it can be appropriate for the uncommitted.

A young couple came to hear their banns read. They kept on coming until the wedding and after it, until they moved out of the district. 'It feels like a family,' said Peter that first Sunday.

There must not be too much emphasis on children if everyone is to feel welcome. Today we have a much wider range of music from which to choose. We do not have to sing children's action choruses. Many of today's songs are simple enough for children to understand.

Children and teenagers can take part in our services in many ways, not just in holding up visual aids or giving out service books. One of our best overhead-projector operators is an eleven-year-old. The words we are singing are moved up at exactly the right time. A fourteen-year-old may play the drums, and a sixteen-year-old may provide trumpet accompaniment to appropriate hymns and songs. Children can contribute their own prayers, and their reading aloud is often better than that of many adults. Many of these things are simply a continuation or a development of aspects of the sixties-style family service.

In other areas the changes are more obvious. We make less use of quizzes and competitions, partly because our world today does plenty to encourage people to compete against one another and little to help them to work together. When we do divide into groups, we try to avoid a 'boys v girls' approach. We want the sexes to appreciate complementing one another, not to compete against one another. We are learning, too, to talk together in small groups during a service, sharing our experience and ideas. Adults are encouraged to listen to children, as well as children to adults. We take the opportunity to greet one another during the service, to indicate our desire to be a family, to accept one another as God accepts us, to share his love, joy and peace.

The talk is no longer aimed at a single age-group, the nine-year-olds or perhaps the twelve-year-olds. It deliberately ranges across the age span of all those present. A simply-put statement of fact will be followed by several illustrations, one with which a child can identify, one for the teenager and another at adult level. A visual aid is as important for the adult as for the child. Today's adults have largely grown up in a world where advertising is strongly visual.

Worshipping as one family together has come to stay. More and more, as we learn to be the church of the nineties, we shall endeavour to bring the generations together. This does not mean the end of activities with people of our own age. Children will still need groups where they can be with their peers, discovering what God can mean to them and worshipping him as a group of children. Yet they also need adults— people of a similar age to their parents and also of the grandparent and great-grandparent generations. 'Inter-generational' is a clumsy word, but one we shall get used to as we explore its reality. Together, across the generations, we shall be learning from one another, nurturing one another. A child's loving concern for the elderly person in the seat in front is just as significant in the life of the church as the adults' desire to pass on to the next generation the news of the great things God has done.[3]

Drawing together, then, all that has been written above, I believe that there is a place in our parochial strategy for including a family service, and for using that title, provided that the service:

1   Draws all present together for all-age worship of God the Father 'from whom his whole family in heaven and on earth derives its name' (Eph 3:15).
2   Provides a fairly simple, but not childish, service where every member of the parish may feel at home, from young children to the elderly and retired, married and single, as a local expression of the family of God. The simplicity of the service will not only mean that it is suitable for children, but also provide a 'bridge' for the unchurched into the worshipping life of the community. It is unlikely, therefore, to be Eucharistic.
3   Provides a suitable service for the nuclear families, who are primarily responsible for the spiritual upbringing of their children, according to the Bible and *Book of Common Prayer*, but obviously need the support and co-operation of the local church to help them do so. Because this may mean bringing babies to church, thought needs to be given to the provision of a creche.

The power of pictures

Margaret Old stressed the great importance of the visual in modern communication. There is an old, wise saying:

> I hear and I forget
> I hear and see and I remember
> I hear and see and do and I understand.

15

Bishop Michael of Chester, who has most kindly written the Foreword to this book, has told me of people who have written to him referring specifically to visual-aid talks that had been so helpful in their Christian life, and which they still remember. I once had the fascinating experience of having the 'dustbin' talk that was published in my *Teaching the Families* (Falcon, 1973) being described to me in great detail by someone who had watched their curate present it *before that book was published!* (Apparently a member of that curate's congregation had seen me give the talk and passed the details on.) I very much doubt if that would have happened if I had only told it, without acting it out.

I gave Steward Symon's talk 'A Tale of Two Oranges' (No 32) at harvest, 1989. My local primary school gave me a pictorial outline some days later. A parent spoke to me about it two months later, because her four-year-old son had so much enjoyed it. A Scout leader asked me if there was any objection to his repeating it at his Scout camp the next summer.

In his book on preaching, *The Sacrament of the Word*, Lord Donald Coggan writes:

> I am aware...that the world of the late twentieth century has passed largely from a word culture into an image culture—the Christian message must be presented visually, by means of drama, television, and so on, if it is to gain access to mind and conscience today.[4]

For this reason visual aids figure very prominently in the talks that follow; they are even suggested by Stephen Trapnell for addresses at weddings. John Anscombe contributes a chapter on video that could become a feature of ministry in church buildings in the nineties.

Rather than repeat chapters that appear in previous books, I have included in the Appendix details about such visual aids as the teazlegraph, overhead projector (OHP) and daylight screen.

No easy option

The Bishop of Taunton, the Right Revd Nigel McCulloch, hit the headlines in the summer of 1989 by describing the sermon he heard on holiday as a 'disgrace'. Writing in the Bath and Wells *Diocesan News*, he said:

The preacher spoke long, but said little. There was no message. As I looked around at my fellow worshippers I could see from the sleeping of the old and the fidgeting of the young that they, like me, were finding the sermon dull, uninspiring and irrelevant. What a lost opportunity. In fact, what a disgrace.[5]

The bishop wondered, as he sat and yawned, what was the point of organising a Decade of Evangelism.

If St Paul were to be asked to advise the Church of England what to do in the Decade of Evangelism, he would tell us what he told Timothy. In every pulpit in every church at every service, 'Preach the Word.'[6]

And this message is just as applicable when giving family-service talks as any others, especially as it is the time when we are likely to have the most people from the margins of the church. As I have said in my previous books, anyone who believes he or she has only to copy down the outlines that follow and make a quick visual aid is doomed to immediate disappointment. The family-service talk is no easy option, but usually requires more prayer and preparation time than more conventional sermons.

In Lord Coggan's book, from which I have already quoted, he lists the major features of the preaching of Jesus, whom Nicodemus described as 'a teacher who has come from God' (Jn 3:2). There was a *winsomeness*, a personal charm about him. There was a *simplicity* about the language he used. He preached with *authority* that was self-authenticating. There was *urgency, positive directiveness* and *respect for the intelligence of his hearers*. His preaching was essentially *God-centred*.[7] May that be our ambition with all our offerings at family services.

Rural ministry

The very day I received my copy of *For All the Family* in November 1984, I moved into rural ministry combined with sector ministry responsibility. My two united parishes had never heard of family services, and I seriously wondered if there would be any place for them, because families were thin on the ground. However, a Christingle service on Christmas Eve rapidly changed my mind: parents and children came out of the woodwork, and within a few months monthly family services were established at both churches.

The numbers attending quickly exceeded those normally found at the more traditional services, and this proved extremely important at one church, where the traditionalists, who were already well catered for, also wanted to have the service stopped and replaced by Morning Prayer from the *Book of Common Prayer*. I told the Parish Council that if that was what members really wanted, I would conform. However, they needed to appreciate that the congregation would likely drop by two-thirds, so would the offertory; and all those new people, who we were seeing in church for the first time would swell the other church's congregation. We still have our family service in both churches!

Obviously rural churches cannot have the sophistication associated with those in suburbia or the city-centre, but we now use a wide range of visual aids, have some singing to a guitar group, have families leading the prayers and conclude with refreshments in church.

Another factor must not be overlooked in this situation, namely that family services can be led by lay readers and deacons, thus freeing the over-stretched clergyman to celebrate at Communion services at other churches in the parish, or even to be away on some other ministry.

My prayer is that during this Decade of Evangelism family services may continue to harvest the 'unchurched', and that the talks that follow may be used by God's Spirit to help further the preaching of the Word.

Michael Botting
Editor

Notes

1 Gloria Durka, quoted in *Children in the Way* (NS/CHP: London, 1988), 3.15, p 30.
2 *Patterns For Worship* (CHP: London, 1989), p 3.
3 From private correspondence with the author, used with permission.
4 Donald Coggan, *The Sacrament of the Word* (Collins: London, 1987), p 14.

5 Quoted in the *Church Times*, 1st September 1989, p 3.
6 *Ibid.*
7 Coggan, *op cit*, pp 53–8.

Using Videos With Large Groups

The queues for the best seats at the Cup Final were amazing. They started soon after breakfast for a 3pm kick-off. And that was just to watch the game on television! The television lounge in our student hall of residence was filled to bursting, and despite the fact that people at the back could hardly see the screen (let alone the pictures on it), a great time was had by all.

That student Cup Final audience was committed to what it was seeing, and each person there had made an individual decision to watch. Furthermore, they didn't have to worry about absorbing complex ideas or following an argument or plot, and they all knew the form a televised football match takes (ie they knew what to expect). The result was that their background knowledge and their desire to see the game and to enjoy the party atmosphere overcame all the difficulty and discomfort occasioned by 150 people all trying to watch the one television.

But the average church audience watching a 'Christian video' is very different. Very few of them will have chosen the video they are watching—leaders will have done that for them. Very few, if any, will have a personal stake in what is on the screen (unless a friend or relative is featured). And the material they are watching will probably require a far greater level of concentration than a football match (and will not follow such a predictable course). So, to expect fifty or more of them to absorb the programme and its content while watching a tiny distant screen and hearing distorted sound is asking an awful lot.

So what can be done (short of handing out binoculars with the hymn books) to enable a large number of people (fifty or more) to watch a single programme? A number of alternatives all have their advantages and disadvantages:

1 *Use a film instead*

Advantages: A large, bright, projected image.

A sense of being involved in a communal activity as everyone watches the same screen.

Disadvantages: Total black-out is needed.

The range of available films is far smaller than that for video.

Films are much more expensive to buy and to hire than video.

A film requires an experienced projectionist.

2 *Multi-monitor video*

The linking of a number of television sets or video monitors to a single video recorder.

Advantages: Programmes can be shown in daylight.

It is comparatively cheap and can make use of readily available equipment.

Disadvantages: It fragments the audience, who are no longer united by a single screen.

Considerable effort is needed to get together all the monitors or televisions, the stands on which to place them, and all the cables and plugs, and then to connect everything together in such a way that people don't trip over the cables or knock over the monitors.

3 *Integral video projector and screen system*

This system has its own built-in concave screen on to which the picture is projected. It is a large, cumbersome piece of equipment with a screen which can be anything from 3 to 5 ft wide. It looks rather like an old-fashioned radiogram with a screen attached!

Advantages: Everyone watches the same screen.

Disadvantages: Black-out is required.
Professional expertise is needed to set up the equipment.
Unless one is sitting directly in front of the screen, straight lines in the picture start to curve and the colour begins to fade. The greater the angle to the screen, the greater the distortion and colour-fading.
It is difficult to move around.
It is expensive.

4   *Video projector*
This system projects on to an ordinary flat screen (the sort used for projecting slides—although you might want to hire a larger one).

Advantages: Everyone watches the same screen.
A large, bright, projected image (as large as your screen).

Disadvantages: Black-out is required.
Professional expertise is needed to set up the equipment every time it is moved—even the shortest distance.
The projector has to be close to the screen, so people cannot sit directly behind it.
It is expensive.

Organising a multi-monitor or multi-television showing

It is important to understand the difference between a monitor and a television set.

A monitor receives the picture and sound signals from the video recorder through two separate wires. The picture signal comes from the 'video out' socket of the video recorder through a coaxial cable usually ending in either a 'BNC' or 'phono' plug. The sound comes from the 'audio out' socket through a two-core audio cable ending in any one of three different plugs: a 'miniature jack', a 'phono' or a 'DIN'.

It is essential that any monitor you borrow or hire has a 'loop facility' (most of them do) which allows the signals from the video recorder not only to enter the monitor, but also to be passed on to another monitor.

The picture quality of a monitor is slightly better than that of a television set.

A television set receives the picture and sound signals together through a single 'RF lead' from the video recorder into the aerial socket of the television.

To send the signal from the video recorder to more than one television, you need a series of 'Y-connectors' (one for each extra television set). The base of the 'Y' is plugged into the television-aerial socket, and the RF lead from the video recorder is plugged into one of the arms of the 'Y'. Then another RF lead goes from the other arm of the 'Y' into the next television set (either directly into the aerial socket, or into another 'Y').

When arranging for a multi-set showing, it is important to establish what kinds of sets you are getting (monitors or televisions), what connections and sockets they will need, and how much cable you will need to run round all the sets in such a way that people won't trip over them.

The sets must be mounted in sturdy, safe stands which are sufficiently high for everybody to be able to see clearly.

You may be able to cobble together enough television sets from friends, but you will almost certainly have to buy long RF leads and Y connectors. In practice, although it costs more, you may find it far easier to hire a complete outfit. You may be able to get these through your local high-street television-rental firms—they're worth trying first, but you will probably have to end up contacting specialist suppliers. Look up 'Video Equipment Suppliers' in the *Yellow Pages*.

The likely cost for a two-27″ monitor show (at the time of writing) would be roughly £105: £30 per monitor, £30 (per) for delivery and collection and £7.50 per stand. Outside London, prices could be lower.

Organising a video-projector show

For an important occasion when you can afford it, you will very probably have to go to specialist video-equipment suppliers who will both deliver and set up the equipment. Adjusting the projector takes time, and you should allow a minimum of an hour for the technician to do this. You may also need a separate sound amplifier and loud speakers.

Black-out is essential, otherwise the results are disappointing. When using the separate projector and screen system, you must take great care to see that no one can move the projector or kick the screen—otherwise that hour's work adjusting the projector can be wasted in a moment.

When setting out the room, remember that video pictures are fuzzy pictures; the bigger the screen, the fuzzier the picture! So don't sit anybody too close to the screen. An ideal situation is where the screen takes up the same proportion of the field of vision as a normal television set does for the viewer at home.

If you're using the integral projector and screen system, you need to imagine a line going down the room at right angles to the screen. The audience needs to sit within an angle of no more than 30 degrees either side of that line; otherwise the picture will look very dim.

The likely cost for hiring a video projector could come to £180. To that one has to add roughly £70 for set-up, and £30 for delivery and collection. Again, prices outside London would probably be lower.

John Anscombe
Scripture Union

Teamwork

Is your family service the product of the thinking of one person (perhaps with the aid of this book) or a team of people? We may use someone to read the Bible or lead the intercessions. A music group may lead praise, and we don't normally attempt to play the organ ourselves. But much of this activity may be by delegating various parts of the service rather than by drawing on the resources of a *team* to plan the service.

If you have a monthly family service, it really can help to draw together an ad hoc team of the preacher and about three others. It is useful to meet at least a fortnight in advance, perhaps longer. The nearer your meeting is to the service itself, the less valuable it becomes. The preacher brings to the meeting a rough outline of his talk, preferably with copies for all, together with a few ideas for other parts of the service. The team then works at it.

What are the advantages of this way of working?

1 *It encourages one (or forces one!) to plan ahead*
  If you regard the family service talk as a simple talk, hurriedly thought up on Saturday night, then think again! How nice to get to Saturday night knowing it is all done! The deadline by which your initial preparation must be done becomes the Tuesday evening two and a half weeks beforehand, because you have arranged with your team to meet that night. It doesn't matter if you haven't thought everything through at that stage. In fact, that could be an advantage.

2 *It tests the talk*

If you think you have 'a word from the Lord' which cannot be questioned, then this method is not for you. If you think you always have the best way of presenting Christian truth to all ages, then this method is not for you. But if you genuinely believe that other people can make a real contribution to how the truth is presented, then this is a practical way of allowing that to happen. How?

(a) If your team does not understand your talk, then it is unlikely the congregation will! However certain we may be of what we are saying, our hearers may get a completely different idea. If your 'hearers' are in the first instance a small team, you can think through together a clearer way of saying something. Clergy training has sometimes involved sermon classes, when a group of fellow students listens to a sermon being preached and gives appropriate feed-back. The way suggested here gives the feed-back beforehand and should improve the preaching.

(b) The outline given to the team can actually ask questions: 'What is the best way to illustrate this point?' 'Can we use some drama here?' 'What can we do to involve the younger children?' 'How can this point be explained in one word on a flash card?' The preacher does not necessarily come to the meeting with all the answers.

(c) There must be a recognition that the original outline presented can be challenged. Some lay people are reluctant to challenge the way their minister has put things. Some vicars are reluctant to accept such challenges! The way in which a talk comes out of a meeting may be radically different from the way it went in. One talk which went into the meeting as various objects to be held up to illustrate successive points, came out as a huge tree to be 'grown' in church!

(d) We must accept that the preacher does not have a mono-poly of the inspiration of the Holy Spirit. The refining work of the Holy Spirit may well be present through other members of the team. Such refining work may result in a better talk.

3   *It teaches the team*
   (a)   The children's evangelist, R. Hudson Pope, used the phrase from 2 Tim 2:2 (RSV), 'To teach others also', as a title for his book on spiritual work with children (CSSM, 1953). In that verse Timothy is told to take the teachings from Paul and to entrust them to reliable people who will be able to teach others also. There are four learners in Paul's process. Truths learned by Paul go to Timothy, then to reliable people, then to others. Gathering a team together and looking at your talk enables them to learn the truths of that talk for themselves. They, in turn, teach others. So, regardless of how ever few people subsequently learn from the talk when given at the family service, a small team should have learned through the discussion at the planning meeting.

   (b)   The members of the team also learn about planning services. If you include choosing appropriate hymns or songs in your planning, the team learn what kind of songs to use at different points in the service and to look at the appropriateness of the words. The learning is by no means all one way. Often a member of the team discovers just the right hymn, which has not come to the mind of the preacher. Practical lessons are also learned. These include developing a theme for the intercessions, arranging the structure of a service to get a smooth flow or even where to fit in the notices.

4   *It draws on wide resources*
   (a)   Visual aids fall into various categories, but a team can share the responsibility for finding them. What happens when lots of dolls dressed in blue or pink are needed? One member of the team could gather them together from various sources and dress them appropriately. That is much better than the vicar spending many hours collecting and dressing dolls! (If you illustrate throwing boys into the

River Nile in the story of Moses in this way, make sure the unbreakable ones are the 'boys'!)

Someone in your team may know just where to find a syringe, crash-helmet, Polaroid camera, gas-mask or whatever else you need but don't possess yourself.

(b) Some visual aids need to be made. Some preachers are blessed with one gifted person who will make visual aids. That is great. But that person also gets overworked. It can sometimes mean that the visual aids tend to be the same type. The use of a team can bring in a variety of skills: cutting out, lettering, model making. Not all making of visual aids has to be complicated. Simply gathering together lots of cardboard boxes to build a wall requires resourcefulness and transport more than artistic skill.

(c) Some visual aids are people. People of all nations worshipping God in heaven can be depicted by the whole primary-age Sunday school with appropriate dressing-up clothes. Advanced planning with at least one of the teachers on the team and perhaps the help of a few parents can achieve this. You may need an adult dressed up as a famous television interviewer (with appropriate signature tune), a bin man, Father Christmas or something else. The team meeting can plan it.

On one occasion a tramp came to church and sat near the front. Some people didn't bother to welcome him— they thought he was a regular member of the congregation dressed as a tramp to take part in the service! Some even conjectured as to which regular member it was!

(d) Drama is another helpful visual aid. Often it has to be specially written, or at least found. The team can discuss this and some take responsibility for organising it. (See Appendix for ideas.)

Members of the team don't have to do all the work either. They can also share it with others! Far too often in family services we restrict the 'work' to the preacher, who finds or makes all his own visual aids (sometimes inadequately), when it could be a shared task. Meanwhile, the time saved can be used to get going on thinking, in advance, about the next family service!

5 *It involves people 'up front' at family services*

Those who are reading the Bible or leading intercessions are able to play their part with an awareness of the whole service and what it involves, not just their own little bit. This can be particularly helpful in preparing intercessions. People will often volunteer at a team meeting to be involved in particular ways in a service. They feel more comfortable as part of a team and might not have agreed such involvement if asked as an individual. Involvement need not mean a speaking part. Moving props can be an important part of the teamwork for someone who prefers not to speak in public. A person not willing to lead all the intercessions may be willing to lead one prayer as part of a group of people.

Having people 'up front' may help the spiritual development of the individual concerned. It may also have further value in that different members of the congregation may feel they relate to different participants, thereby giving the congregation a greater sense of involvement.

6 *It creates an integrated family service*

Do the various parts of your family service relate to each other—hymn, songs, prayer, readings, talk, quiz, etc? Or is it difficult to see how one part relates to another? Although a team will not automatically guarantee that all items relate to one another, it will make cohesion more likely. Many participants create a disjointed service, but the team meeting again helps to prevent this.

One vital tool for such a family service is an order-of-service sheet. Every participant should have a copy, and it should indicate clearly who does what and when. This enables people not only to know their own part but everyone else's.

7 *It deepens fellowship*

It would be possible simply to ask different groups in the church to form the team, but an ad hoc team for each family service seems to have certain advantages. It means one can have varied contributions. Some may be chosen because they have particular skills to offer for that family service, such as music, drama or artistic ability. Others represent an area of church life, such as Sunday-school teacher or toddler-group parent. Parents are often realistic and have knowledge of the kind of interests their own children have, the television programmes they watch, and the level of children's participation possible. The ad hoc team means, too, that a new member can be brought in alongside more experienced members.

In practice it is good to have a list of names of possible people from which one eventually makes up the team. People often seem to 'be away that week-end' or 'can't come that night for a planning meeting'. It is useful to keep a list of the dates people have been on the team to avoid constantly asking the same people.

Working together in small groups is good for the fellowship of the church. People who might not normally have found themselves working together do so. Having ad hoc teams means those working together change month by month. The need for visual aids can lead to the discovery of the interests, hobbies or jobs of people (or even their friends and relatives). A cross-section of the church working in this way over the age and sex divide can be a helpful way of deepening fellowship between members.

There is increasing emphasis today on the use of gifts and shared ministry. The family service provides an ideal opportunity to put that sharing into practice. If the practices and principles above are applied, they could enable many members of the church family over a period of time to share in the ministry of family services.

Alan Pugmire
Manchester

How To Use Bible Crosswords

A crossword puzzle using Bible words is not a new idea; they have been appearing regularly in a great diversity of Christian publications for as long as I can remember. Nearly all the examples I have come across, however, have been one or other of two types: (1) a symmetrical puzzle, sometimes a shape other than the traditional square, ie a Christmas tree, where the words have no particular connection with each other except that they appear in the Bible; or (2) an irregular arrangement of words, which may or may not be connected closely, in which the blanks are ignored and the completed puzzle looks like a game of Scrabble.

In the crosswords that follow, I have attempted to achieve two particular things: firstly, to devise a puzzle that looks like a traditional crossword, ie it is square or rectangular, and although irregular, it has as few blank squares, and as many overlaps as possible; and, secondly, to have a definite theme rather than a collection of unconnected words.

Of the examples given in this book, most fall into the category of Bible-story puzzles: there are no traditional clues to be unravelled; instead the Bible story is shown under the crossword with the number (across or down, as appropriate) inserted in the text for the missing word. As the story unfolds, the correct words are entered in the grid until the puzzle is complete. (The similarities with the television game *Blankety Blank* are obvious and should be familiar to almost everyone—even the few households that do not possess a television!)

These puzzles are primarily intended for use at family services in the place where a passage from the Bible is normally read. As outlined above, the speaker tells the story, pausing at each blank until a member of the congregation comes up with the correct missing word. It should be appreciated that telling a Bible story in this way takes considerably longer than normal, and so an allowance for this should be built into the timing of the service. The solving of the puzzle as the story is told may, of course, be amplified by comments and illustrations from the speaker, so that it becomes the sermon in the service: the key words (which might, in other presentations, be attached to a display-board) being written in the crossword in a different colour, or highlighted in some other appropriate way.

The remaining puzzles are based on particular verses: all the words of that scripture are contained in the grid; in one puzzle, clues (of a traditional type) are provided only for the additional words that fill the remainder of the grid; in the other example, there are clues for all the words. (See Talks 26 and 46.)

Those puzzles which are based on a single verse are, perhaps, more easily incorporated into the talk. Begin by getting the congregation to solve the clues for those words which are *not* part of the verse; then solve the clues for those words in the verse which are less important. And, finally, identify the key words, which, again, should be highlighted in a different colour, taking care to explain their meaning so that the message of the verse is clearly understood. It may be helpful to write the verse in full under the puzzle, word by word, as it is completed, but do leave sufficient space for words that are dealt with out of their correct order. A line of blank squares may be drawn in advance, thus:

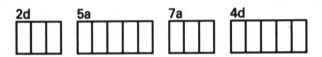

Three other ways in which these puzzles may be used are given below (you may, of course, be able to think of others):

1 They may be done by someone working alone as an entertaining way of learning a Bible story.

2   They can be used as a group activity in Sunday school or Pathfinder group.
3   They could be given to everyone in a class as a Bible-knowledge test.

As far as presentation is concerned, the best method to use with a group or congregation is to project the grid on to a screen by means of an OHP. Alternatively, the grid may be copied for distribution in the service, using a 5mm/¼″ marker, on to as large a piece of paper as possible. (Please see copyright notice on page iv of this book.)

Anybody who finds these puzzles useful will inevitably use them all with his or her congregation (although, to avoid boredom, that should take years!) or find that the themes I have worked out are not the ones they want for a particular occasion. They will also soon discover the weaknesses and limitations of my inspiration! Then perhaps they may wish to invent some crosswords of their own. If so, for guidance, here are the steps to follow.

(a)   Choose a Bible story or verse.
(b)   Make a list of all the key words if you have chosen a story; if a verse is chosen (it should not be more than twenty-five words long—shorter if most of the words have more than five letters), then each and every word in that verse should be listed.
(c)   Next, underline alternate letters of each word in such a way as to give most vowels, eg: S̲A̲M̲A̲R̲I̲T̲A̲N̲ gives _A_A_I_A_. These letters should, as far as possible, be used at crossover points, eg:

(d)   By trial and error (this is where patience and inspiration are required!), fit as many of the key words together, but remember to keep to an overall limit of approximately 200 squares (ie 14x14 or 15x13).

(e) The next stage is to look for synonyms of as many of the remaining key words as possible to fit around those you already have.

(f) To fill the remainder of the grid, a laborious search through the dictionary may be necessary to find suitable words to fit into the story: it may also be necessary to include asides and digressions here (see, for example, Talk 77), but a confident presentation to your audience will invariably hide such weaknesses! NB: it is seldom possible to include *all* the words in your list of key words; those you do include, however, should as far as possible be evenly spread out through the narrative.

(g) Words of two or three letters that do not belong in the story, such as LO, TOY, UP, WE, ERE, ME, AYE, etc, may be ignored if all their letters are included in other words, for example:

Alternatively, they may be written in the grid to start with (and thereby help the participants).

David McIntosh
Ellesmere Port

34

PART ONE
The Christian Year

1 Advent: In Heaven

Rev 7:9–12.

AIM

To show what it will be like in heaven.

PREPARATION

Groups of people need to be prepared beforehand. Angels (suitably dressed), elders (we used the robed choir!), enormous crowd (small children from Sunday school) dressed in different national costumes, eg Japanese, Chinese, African, Swedish, Scottish, Arabian, Russian, Spanish, French, American, Canadian (cowboy), Red Indian. It depends on availability of costumes or ideas for improvisation.

Also needed are crib, wooden cross, robe with words 'King of kings and Lord of lords'.

PRESENTATION

Assuming it will take place during Advent, ask if you can see anything in windows of people's homes reminding you of Christmas. (Christmas tree.) Therefore, you get a look at part of their Christmas activity and celebrations. At first Christmas there was celebration in heaven. We are going to have a look at what celebration in heaven might be like in future.

People there

1 *Angels*
    (Gather children dressed as angels together.) At Christmas we know that angels were seen by shepherds. Sang 'Glory to God in the highest heaven'. The look into heaven given to us by John in last book of Bible is one in which we see angels.

37

2 *Elders*

(Gather your elders round to join angels.) Could be angels or just 'God's people'. That includes those from long time ago. Some would be born and would have died before we were born. Some would be famous. Others would not be well-known.

3 *Four living creatures*

You could try to depict them or indicate they are impossible to describe, but remind us that God is the creator of everything.

4 *Enormous crowd*

(Bring on children of different lands.) You can do this by mentioning the nations and getting an assistant (probably who helped to dress the children) to send on the right child at right time. Get over the message that it will be a worldwide gathering. We have them dressed differently, but Bible says they will have white robes (all alike). You can add holding palm branches if you wish. Don't expect everyone to speak English in heaven!

Sing: You could have a time of worship here using songs that are about heaven or worship in heaven.

Reading: Rev 7:9–12.

Person worshipped

Explain that in heaven all these people will come together to worship. Who? God. Verse 10 tells us why they worship. Salvation.

(a) *Crib*

(Show your crib.) When Christ came as baby, he was called 'Jesus'. What does it mean? 'Saviour'. Therefore, we can worship God and thank him that Jesus gives us salvation.

(b) *Cross*

(Show your cross—possibly coming from crib.) Thirty-three years later. Another picture of worship in heaven (Rev 5:12 GNB) is of a 'Lamb who was killed'. Before the days of Jesus, a lamb was killed instead of people, so that people might receive forgiveness of sin. When Jesus died on the cross, he was like that lamb sacrificed. It is possible for us to be forgiven. Therefore, he is worshipped in heaven as the Lamb who died.

(c) He is not still dead. He is alive. He has gone into heaven as

King. He wears a robe (put robe round cross) saying, 'King of kings and Lord of lords' (Rev 19:16). He is, therefore, more important than the Queen, the President of the USA or USSR, or any king anywhere in the world.

Sing: You could have more worship here (eg 'King of kings and Lord of lords').

Kind of worship

How do we celebrate Christmas? We celebrate birthdays the same way. Parties! Heaven will be a kind of party. It is described as 'the wedding-feast of the Lamb' (Rev 19:9 GNB). At that wedding-feast, Christ is like bridegroom and all Christians (elders, enormous crowd) like bride. Christians will one day join together in that worship. Our worship here on earth is a kind of practice for it!

You can end with a party atmosphere with lively worship songs, streamers and dancing! It's a practice for heaven!

Alan Pugmire
Manchester

2 Advent: Getting Ready

TEXT

Mt 24:44.

AIM

To show the need to be ready when Jesus returns.

PREPARATION

You will need:

1 An ark. One side can be depicted by cardboard supported from behind.
2 Water. A blue cloth on the floor can be used to indicate water rising.
3 Umbrella(s).
4 Table with food and drink.
5 Two people dressed as bride and groom and some guests.
6 Two people dressed as farmers.
7 Two housewives with bowls, etc, to prepare food.
8 Children to be Noah, Mrs Noah, Shem, Ham and Japheth and their wives. Children dressed up as various animals (two of each), or carrying pictures of animals.

PRESENTATION

Noah

Begin with reference to 'getting ready' for Christmas (or other event if at different time of year). We are going to think about a man who got ready: Noah. What did he do? Built a boat. (Have helpers to lift up your 'boat'.)Other people thought he was mad. Long way from anywhere he could sail it, but he said God had told him to build it.

   Took people into boat (as you say, get them to come into boat).

Mr Noah, wife, Mrs Noah, sons, Shem, Ham and Japheth, their wives, Mrs Shem, Mrs Ham and Mrs Japheth. Lots of animals went in two by two. (Name them as they go in. Get your organist to play 'The animals went in two by two' as background.)

Meanwhile, others didn't go in the boat. People were married (bride and groom come to table). They had their guests at their party (guests join them). They thought Noah was silly taking all those people in the boat.

But then (put hand out to test if raining), it began to rain (umbrella(s) up). Rain came down. Floods came up. (Helpers lift blue cloth up and down as if waves.) People in ark were safe. People not in the ark were drowned (all at table fall to floor—or off). 'They did not realise what was happening until the Flood came and swept them all away' (Mt 24:39 GNB).

Son of Man

'That is how it will be when the Son of Man comes' (v 39 GNB). Who is the Son of Man? Jesus. He has gone away to heaven. He is coming back to earth one day. We don't know when. Some people think it is silly to get ready for his return, so they carry on with life. They don't bother about what God says. They don't bother about what God's people say. Enjoy life. Carry on with all the normal things, like being married.

Two men will be working in field (bring two farmers on). When Jesus comes, one will be taken to be with him (one farmer off). The other will be left. Difference is that one had taken notice of God. Like Noah, he lived with a trust in and obedience to God. He went to be with Jesus. Other had not bothered about God. He was left in the world, even as people were left out of the boat in Noah's day and destroyed by Flood.

Two women will be grinding at the mill (housewives come on). Explain same kind of thing happening to them as to the farmers. When Jesus returns, will you be ready? Or will you be left? It will be like the time of Noah. The ones who were ready were in the ark. The ones who were not ready were destroyed. End with text: Mt 24:44.

Alan Pugmire
Manchester

3 Bible Sunday: How To Read the Bible

TEXT

2 Tim 3:14–17 (GNB).

AIM

A practical plan on how to read the Bible.

PREPARATION

Use an OHP. You will need either (a) four pictures revealed in sequence on one screen (use an acetate frame with four non-trans-parent windows that open up in sequence to reveal four pictures below on a separate acetate) or (b) four pictures put separately on to screen; then single picture of two drinks.

Four-window cover frame

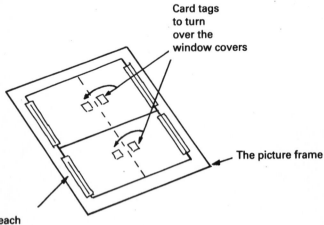

Card tags
to turn
over the
window covers

The picture frame

Hinge each
of the four window covers to the
picture frame

Lay the window cover frame over the top of a separate frame that holds the pictures to be shown. Check alignment and secure with hinges, as shown.

PRESENTATION

Introduction

We live in a day of 'how to' books. (Give, and possibly show, examples.) When it comes to reading the Bible, we can benefit from both a *method* and a *motivation* in regularly reading the scriptures.

Here are four basic steps

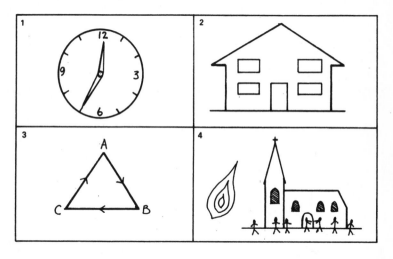

1   *Regular time (show first picture)*
    Explain the advantages of a set time each day. This applies to when you read and for how long. Allow for personal variation according to different people and circumstances: before/after breakfast, mid-morning lunch, afternoon break, bedtime.
2   *Regular place (show second picture)*
    This can be wherever you feel at ease and free from interruption. It may be your bedroom, the kitchen, the sitting-room, somewhere near where you work.

3 *Regular routine (show third picture)*

This can apply to either an individual, a couple, or a family. Endeavour to keep to it; if week-ends throw out the routine, hold to it on weekdays. The routine needs to be one that allows you to reflect upon the Bible reading, remember God in prayer, relax, enjoy and benefit from listening to what God says to you through the scriptures.

4 *Regular guide (show fourth picture)*

The best guide we have to understanding the Bible and hearing what God has to say to us is the Holy Spirit (Jn 16:13–15). By prayer, we can talk to God and ask him to guide us in applying the teaching of the Bible to our daily lives. To assist our understanding, various Christian organisations provide helpful Bible notes. Here are some of them: Bible Reading Fellowship, Bible Society, Scripture Union, Crusade for World Revival.

How much do you read at any one time?

Here are two pictures that may help you to think about this question:

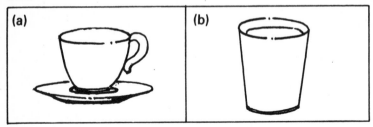

(a) A *short* reading: sip it like tea or wine.
(b) A *long* reading: drink it like lemonade or beer.

Remember the value of various approaches to reading the Bible. If one style is helpful, stick with it, but if you prefer variety, then change at regular intervals to other notes or books.

Our goal is that commended by Paul when writing to Timothy (2 Tim 3:14–17).

Ray Adams
Redditch

4 Bible Sunday: A Sure Foundation

TEXT

Mt 7:24–9; Lk 6:46–9.

AIM

To show how the Bible is a sure foundation for life.

PREPARATION

Select two different black OHP pens, preferably thick. One should be water-soluble and the other permanent. Make ten small pieces of paper, two sets of five. One set with four small squares and a small rectangle. The other set should be identical, but with small buttons of Blu-Tack on the back of each shape.

Mount two blank acetates on to acetate surrounds for stability. Also have ready a small glass of water.

PRESENTATION

Tell the story of the two house builders.

First, the foolish man. Draw a house shape (fig 1) with the soluble pen. You can put some words into his mouth about what a good spot he has discovered for himself: pretty sand to play with, right next to a stream, etc. As you talk, place on to the drawing the shapes without the Blue-Tack (fig 2). Then the wind came (fig 3), and you blow off the shapes (A). After that, the rain came (B), and you can scatter some water droplets on to the soluble ink. You will need to be skilful enough to make a good mess, and not soak the projector!

Second, the wise man. Repeat, the build up. It's always helpful to be repetitive, as in children's story-books. This time, however, use the permanent pen and the shapes with Blu-Tack. When the wind and the rain come, the house stays firm.

Bring out the implications for the word of God.

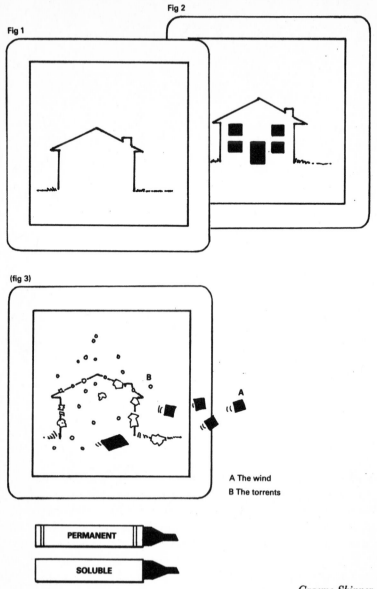

Fig 1

Fig 2

(fig 3)

A The wind
B The torrents

PERMANENT

SOLUBLE

Graeme Skinner
Bebington

5 Bible Sunday: The Sword of the Spirit

TEXT

Eph 6:17; Lk 4:1–13.

AIM

To take hold of the sword of the Spirit.

PREPARATION

Careful drawing on an overhead acetate will help to fix the image of the word of God being a sword in the minds of all present.

One of the acetates needs to be drawn with the letters 'B ble' in the bottom left-hand corner (fig 1). Lay a second acetate over these letters, and in the gap between 'B' and 'b' draw an 'i'. As illustrated, this can be turned into a sword (fig 2). Cut out a border for this second acetate, as shown. Then fix the two board surrounds as shown, in order to allow the acetate with the sword to swing away (fig 3).

Also make or borrow a real sword.

PRESENTATION

Draw on the idea of the word of God as a 'sword'. Use the real sword for a short explanation of what a sword is used for: defending; and attacking. A fencing expert would be a real bonus! Alternatively, use an overhead drawing of a sword, preferably the same as the one that will fill in the 'B ble' illustration.

Refer to Jesus' use of the word of God when he was fighting in the desert. It would be good to see how much people remember without a reading of the Temptations.

The word of God also makes sense of our lives. Put up the 'B ble' acetate, with the sword totally out of the picture. Bring it into view (fig 4). Give a personal explanation of how the Bible has made sense

47

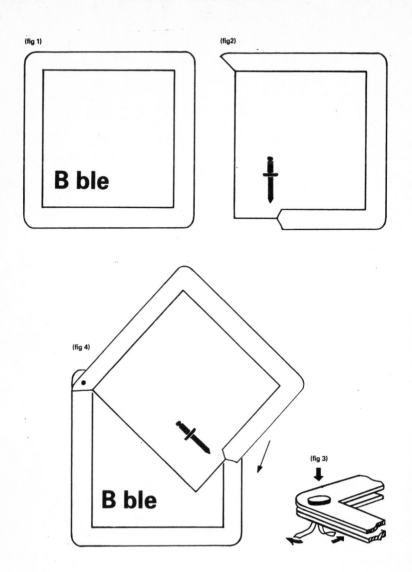

of something for you. After that, swing the sword into position to 'make sense' of the meaningless letters.

End by encouraging people to take hold of the sword. Ask the younger ones how this can be done. Have some examples of Bible-reading notes at hand.

Graeme Skinner
Bebington

6 The Incarnation

Jn 1:1–14.

AIM

To show how the pre-existent Son, the Agent of creation, became the Light, whereby we may become children of God.

PREPARATION

Make the following figures from coloured card or paper. Apart from the 'God' disc, all these can be seen below:

1 Three circles to represent the Trinity with the words 'Father', 'Spirit', 'Word'
2 A disc large enough to cover the Trinity, on which is written 'God'
3 A large disc representing the globe
4 Several smaller pictures of living things, eg birds, trees, flowers, fish, etc
5 Several groups to represent people
6 An arrow
7 A manger which will fit inside the circle representing the Word
8 A large candle which will fit inside the circle representing the Word
9 Two or three smaller candles to be attached to two or three of the 'people'.

PRESENTATION

The visual aid is built up as each verse is expounded.
    (Cover visual aid completely.)
    What existed before the world? Nothing? God! (Uncover to show God.)
    Verse 1a. (Remove 'God' to reveal the Trinity.)
    Verse 1–2. What does it say about the Word?
    Verse 3. Through whom was the world created? (Uncover the globe, and place arrow from Word.)
    Compare with creation story: Gen 1:3, 9, 11, etc. 'God said...'
    Verse 4a. What were some of the living things that were created? (Add trees, flowers, birds, etc, around globe. Add groups of people on globe.)

NB: God the Trinity is in   }   Linked because creation
      heaven. Creation separate.   was through the Word.

    Verse 14a. The Incarnation.
    (Move the circle representing Word and place it on the globe, and put the manger in the centre of the circle.)
    The Creator of the whole world had become a human baby!
    Verse 4b. What else did the Word bring to the world?
    (Replace the manger with the large candle.)
    Verses 6–9. Expound.

Verse 10. Expound, not everyone recognised the Word.

Verse 11. Compare with the innkeeper and others.

Verse 12. Expound.

(Place small candles on several of the people to represent those who receive the Light.)

Judith Rose
Gillingham, Kent

7 Christingle Service: The Light of the World

TEXT

Is 9:2–7 (GNB).

AIM

To show something of what it means to us for Jesus to be the Light of the World.

PREPARATION

Using brightly coloured card or paper, prepare a visual aid to be revealed during the talk. The final effect should look like fig 1. The wording to be filled in using ladder lettering, for which a paint-brush and black powder paint is needed.

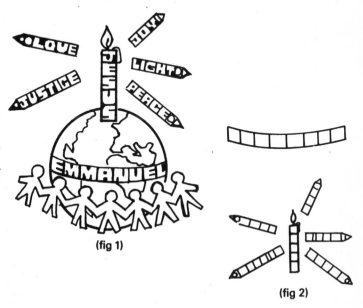

(fig 1)

(fig 2)

Make four large cards on which are the words: 'Wonderful Counsellor', 'Mighty God', 'Eternal Father', 'Prince of Peace'.

PRESENTATION

Talk about darkness and what it signifies: sadness, fear, evil, etc....

Verse 2. 'The people who walked in darkness (explain the background to Is 9) have seen a great light' (uncover fig 2 part of visual aid).

Who or what is the light? The names given in verse 6. (Ask four children to hold up the cards showing the four names.)

Is 7:14 gives us another name. (Uncover and fill in the name Emmanuel.)

Emmanuel means 'God with us'.

NB: the five titles now attributed to the child.

The World. A little light may enlighten a room, but it would need a very, very...big light to enlighten the world. (Uncover the globe.)

What will the light bring? With ladder lettering, fill in each word in turn, and talk about the quality.

Peace. Verse 7a. (Hold up card: Prince of Peace.)

Justice. Verse 7b. (Hold up card: Wonderful Counsellor.)

Love. (Hold up card: Eternal Father.) Talk about self-giving love.

Light and Joy. (Hold up card: Mighty God.) Verses 2b–3. These two qualities are gifts of God: light instead of darkness; joy instead of sadness.

Jesus. This picture was given to Isaiah c 700 BC. Who was to be this great light, the Light of the World? (Fill in the word 'Jesus' on the candle.)

Application

Yet our world does not always show peace, justice, etc.... Has God's plan failed? No. God calls his people to work out his purposes. (Add figures round the world to show our involvement.) We have a responsibility to (a) let the light of Christ shine in our lives; and (b) show his peace, justice, love, etc. To help us, we have Emmanuel—God with us.

Judith Rose
Gillingham, Kent

8   God's Christmas Card

Text

Lk 2:11–12.

Aim

To tell the Christmas story using a fairly elaborate visual aid. The talk is suitable for a Christmas tree or Christingle service.

Preparation

Design a large Christmas card, say 5' by 3'4" or 1.5m x 1m (white card can be purchased from good stationery wholesalers in this size). You'll need two sheets. It is essential if the card is to stand up that it has a wooden frame around its sides and that the join has proper hinges. The inside of the card should show at the top in black script 'To all sinners'. Below it in brightly coloured script put 'Happy Christmas'. The outside of the card could be covered with an attractive Christmas wrapping-paper pasted down. In the lower part cut out a large circular hole 2'9" or 83.5 cm in diameter, the bottom of the hole being about 7.5" or 19 cm from the bottom of the card. When the card is semi-closed, the wording 'Happy Christmas' inside the card should be fully visible through the hole. In the top part of the outside of the card cut out shapes of a cradle to the left, a cross central, and a crown to the right. Coloured day-glo paper— yellow, red and orange respectively—should be stuck over the gaps and the shapes of the cradle, cross and crown fitted back into card, so that they are not evident at the beginning of the talk.

Arrange to have four responsible children dressed up as Mary, Joseph, a shepherd and a king. Provide the shepherd with a fleece. Have a small manger with hay or straw and possibly a light in it that can be lit at the appropriate moment. The four children and the manger should be somewhere close to where the talk is being given, but out of sight. There should be an angle-poise lamp near where the card will be placed, which can later be switched on to light up the inside of the card. Obtain from the Post Office a postman's outfit. I have never had any problem in borrowing one, but you will not be able to borrow a badge, so one will need to be made out of cardboard. Dress up a suitable man who will fit the uniform and ask him to wait outside the room or church where the talk is to be given.

PRESENTATION

Explain the problem a friend of yours had one Christmas when he was handed two Christmas cards to deliver to God and Jesus. Of course, Christmas is a celebration of Jesus' birthday, but it is more about a message from God to us than us to God, so we are going to think about God's Christmas card to us. Explain that every Christmas card must have:

1   *A sender*
    Ask why we send cards? Suggest: because we have always done so; because some people would be offended if we didn't; because we love the person. Agree that the last is the reason why God has sent a message to us, because he loves us.
2   *A deliverer*
    Ask how most cards come to us, and on receiving the reply, 'By the postman,' ask your postman to come in with the card. Discover to whom it is addressed, and on seeing, 'To all sinners', ask who that means. Enlarge on the problem of sin in the world, but stress that we are all to blame. The card should be placed slightly open, but so that the words 'Happy Christmas' are lit by the angle-poise lamp and can be seen by all.
3   *The message*
    It is all about Jesus:
    (a)   *The cradle.* Perhaps explain the problem of making a pet understand what you are saying. You really need to become a dog, so that you can bark the same language! At Christmas God became a man, so that he could speak to us person to person. The Holy Family should come out from the card through the hole, bringing the manger, which should then be lit up. Take the cradle shape from the top of the outside of the card, which will show up because of the light from the angle-poise lamp.
    (b)   *The cross.* Explain that Jesus came to be more than just a

man. Refer to the message of the angels to the shepherds, stressing the word 'Saviour'. The shepherd could come through the card carrying his fleece. Point out that sheep have more than one use. They give us wool, but also something else. Enquire what, and on receiving the answer that they provide lamb or mutton to eat, explain that that means they have to die. Explain that Jesus had to die to be our Saviour, and take out the cross shape from the top of the outside of the card.

(c)   *The crown.* Ask who else came to visit the baby Jesus, and on receiving an answer about kings, the king enters through the card. Explain that Jesus did more than die. He also rose from the dead and ascended to his Father in heaven, where he now reigns. He calls us to make him both Saviour and King of our lives. Take out the crown shape from the top of the outside of the card.

4   *The receiver*

When the postman comes, we don't have to receive our cards. We probably all know someone who's had a card returned! But have we received God's message: the offer of a Saviour and a King?

Postscript

Ask the postman how we know he is one? He shows his badge: that witnesses to his being a real postman. If we have received God's message, we should also be like postmen—delivering the message everywhere. (See Acts 1:8.)

Michael Botting
Editor

9 The Christmas Cake

TEXT

Lk 2:11–12.

AIM

See Talk 8.

PREPARATION

Create a round cake made of cardboard, 'iced' with plaster of Paris and decorated with a small Christmas tree, a Father Christmas and a cracker. In the centre there should be a single candle that can be lit. Have a wide ribbon round the cake, with the words in silver letters 'Christmas Trappings'. This shell of icing should come off the cake, revealing underneath four slices, each a quarter of the cake. Each slice should have the following words on one of the flat sides: JESUS, FRUIT, CHURCH and HOPE. The other flat side of each slice should illustrate respectively: Saviour (cross), Spirit (flames), family (figures of various shapes, sizes and colours) and heaven. Someone dressed up as a chef with large knife can come in with the cake.

PRESENTATION

Ask why have a cake at Christmas. Refer to Jesus' birthday and consider how many candles. Draw out that, of course, he is an eternal Person, being God. Express wonder that despite all the problems of the world, the light of Jesus still burns, and every year people have a chance to be reminded of his coming. However, the trouble is that people have covered the season with so many things that really have nothing to do with Jesus, like Father Christmas, etc. So remove the trappings of Christmas from the cake and see under- neath what it is really all about, getting the chef to appear to be cutting each slice and handing them in turn to the speaker for appropriate comment. Refer to Jesus the Saviour, the gift and fruit of the Spirit, the family of the church and the hope of heaven.

Michael Botting
Editor

10 The Christmas Feast

TEXT

Mt 1:21.

AIM

See Talk 8.

PREPARATION

Dress a family of mother, father, daughter and son in traditional Victorian costume, such as we associate with Dickensian pictures on some Christmas cards. Have a bare table, two large table-cloths—one dirty and with holes, the other 'Persil' white—a papier-maché turkey, a Christmas pudding and a bowl of sweets in large wrappings, so that they are easily seen. Have candles in candlesticks, cutlery and plates.

PRESENTATION

Point out that Christmas is called a feast-day in the Christian calendar, and important to our celebrations is the dinner. We will, therefore, illustrate the real meaning of Christmas by means of a Victorian Christmas dinner.

Mother comes on with her dirty table-cloth and is about to lay the table with it. Point out that the great feast to which the world is moving, though not all will attend, is the heavenly banquet given by God the Father in honour of his Son, and to which God has given each one of us here an open invitation. But only the pure can come. God cannot accept any at his table with any black mark or impurity, because heaven is a perfect place. One speck of sin and heaven would be spoiled.

Hand mother the clean table-cloth. She sets the table and lights the candles. Point out that none of us are clean and fit for God's feast, because we are sinners. But the good news is that God has made a way for us to be accepted at his table.

Let us see what is on God's menu. Father brings on the turkey and the point is made that the only reason why it can be enjoyed is because it had to die. Refer to Mt 1:21 and speak of the death of Jesus, that he could become our Saviour.

The daughter brings on the Christmas pudding. Often they are brought on flaming. Speak of the Holy Spirit, who came with tongues of fire. Fire purifies. Puddings are made with fruit. The Holy Spirit has come to give us his fruit of love, joy, peace...all the things that we talk about at Christmas, but only Christians can know in reality.

Finally, the son comes on with the bowl of sweets. Refer to a famous advert about some well-known brand 'made for sharing'. If we have really begun to taste of God's feast, then we should want to share it with others who have not.

Michael Botting
Editor

11 Christmas Story
(a crossword talk on Lk 2:1–16 GNB)

At that time the Emperor Augustus ordered a census to be taken throughout the 9 across (5) Empire. A 4 down (3) called 12 down (6) went from the town of 20 across (8) in Galilee, to the town of 6 down (9) in 11 down (6). He went to register with 19 down (4), who was promised in marriage to him. While they were there, the time came for her to have her 22 across (4). She gave birth to her first-born son, wrapped 23 across (3) in strips of cloth and laid him in a 4 across (6); there was no 18 down (4) for them to stay in the inn.

There were some shepherds in that part of the country who were spending the night in the fields, taking care of their 1 across (6). An angel of the 2 down (4) appeared to them, and the glory of the 2 down (4) shone over them. They were terribly afraid, but the angel said to them,

> Don't be afraid! I am here with 5 down (4) news for you, which will bring great joy to all the people. This very 7 across (3) in the city of 7 down (5) your 14 across (7) was born — 3 down (6)

the Lord. You will find the baby wrapped in strips of cloth and lying in a <u>4 across</u> (6).

Suddenly, a great army of heaven's angels appeared, singing praises to God, a <u>21 across</u> (7) for <u>16 across</u> (4): 'Glory to <u>10 across</u> (3) in the highest heaven, and <u>13 down</u> (5) <u>8 across</u> (2) <u>17 across</u> (5) to those with whom he is pleased.' When the angels went away from them back into heaven, the shepherds said to one another, 'Let's go to Bethlehem and see this thing that has happened which the Lord has told us.' So they hurried on <u>15 down</u> (5) and found Mary and Joseph and saw the baby lying in the manger.

David McIntosh
Ellesmere Port

Christmas Story (Lk 2:1 – 16 GNB)

12   New Year's Eve

TEXT

Ps 31:14–16; Eccles 3:1–8; Eph 5:15–17; Rev 22:13.

AIM

To understand that time speaks to us of God's providence and God's purpose in our lives.

PREPARATION

You will require:

1   Party hats
2   A large battery clock.

PRESENTATION

1   *New Year's Eve celebrations (party hats)*
    Elaborate on the ways people celebrate the passing of the old year and the coming of the new. Parties, customs from different countries (eg, Hogmanay in Scotland), bells ringing the old year out and the new year in, boats hooting on the rivers, cars on the roads, etc.
2   *Time moves on (battery clock)*
    Set the clock at 12.00 without the battery, and then put the battery in the clock. The point is that time does not stand still, so how do we make the best use of our time?

    We live by the clock today; indeed, we are a clock-watching people, controlled by its movement for every moment. A time to: get up; go to work/school; eat our breakfast, lunch, dinner, tea-breaks; return home from work/school; go out shopping, play sport, visit people; go to bed. These can be amplified by contributions from the children and adults to personalise the movement of time. Compare Eccles 3:1–8.

3 *What does the Bible teach us about time?*

(a) *God is the Lord of time*

This is true of God in creation, redemption and Second Coming. Rev 22:13.

(b) *God loves us and cares for us at all times*

We experience the providence of God over our lives and within our lives. Ps 31:14–16.

(c) *God calls us to use our time wisely*

To come to him (2 Cor 6:2)

To follow him (Eph 5:15–17)

To serve him (Josh 24:14–15).

Various people could read out the verses of scripture as required. This gives a voice change, involves people and highlights the scriptures.

Ray Adams
Redditch

13 New Year: Time

Ps 90:9–10, 12; Deut 32:7; Rom 13:11; 2 Cor 6:2 (suitable for use with RSV or NIV, but not GNB).

Aim

To remind people to make a wise use of their time.

Preparation

You will need:

1 Watch or timer that you can see (not hear)
2 'Tombstone' recording a person who died aged seventy years
3 Diary, alarm-clock, egg-timer (or timer which indicates 'time up').

Presentation

Begin with everyone standing. Say you want people to sit down after exactly one minute (without looking at watches), or you can get a group of volunteers to do this. Note who wins. You might give them a tiny reward. Say time is divided up into sections, like minutes. God gives each of us a lifetime, which is a number of years to live in the world.

After a person's life, this time span is sometimes written on a tombstone (show it) in years. Bible tells us 'we finish our years' (Ps 90:9) and how many years we might have: 70 or 80 (v 10). (If you have any tombstones or plaques around your church, you could get people to discover how many years they lived. If you have a grave-yard, you could also get children who arrive early to go round and write down how many years people lived.) New Year is a useful reminder that we are getting nearer the end of our years. Quote these lines from an old prayer card:

Only one life, 'twill soon be past,
Only what's done for Christ will last.

One day we will 'finish our years'. How will we have spent them? Every new year some people get something into which they write dates and appointments. What? Diary—divided into months, weeks and days. Bible says, 'Remember the days of old...' (quote Deut 32:7). At New Year some people look back to the past and 'days of old'. (You could do some calculations on how old your church is in days or how many days make up a certain number of years.) It is good to look back to 'days of old'. Fathers and grandmothers can help us by telling us this and explaining things. But remember, when we get to next New Year, we will have had 365 more days to look back on. How will we spend those days? How will we remember them?

Something many people don't like to hear is alarm-clock. Tells us what hour it is. It is the hour to get up. Rom 13:11: 'The hour has come for you to wake up from your slumber.' When clock goes in morning, what do you think of? Not usually past, but future. What am I going to do today? New Year is time to look forward. Paul told people in looking to future to 'clothe yourselves with the Lord Jesus Christ, and do not think about how to gratify the desires of the sinful nature' (Rom 13:14). Live for Jesus, not selves, every hour of this year.

We sometimes want to time things not for hours but minutes, may therefore use an egg-timer. Tells one when minutes are up. Tells one about eggs that 'now is the time!' 2 Cor 6:2: 'Now is the time of God's favour, now is the day of salvation.' God gives people opportunities to receive salvation—to receive Jesus into their lives as Saviour. Now is the time—this minute, at beginning of New Year.

Summarise points reusing visual aids. They all also mention days:
Ps 90:9: 'All our days pass away.'
Deut 32:7: 'Remember the days of old.'
Rom 13:12: 'The night is nearly over; the day is almost here.'
2 Cor 6:2: 'Now is the day of salvation.'
If actually on New Year's Day, you can stress significance and opportunity of New Year's Day as 'day of salvation'.

Alan Pugmire
Manchester

14   Christmas VIPs (Wise Men and the Escape to Egypt)

TEXT

Mt 2:1–17.

AIM

To contrast the different VIPs involved in the birth story of Jesus recorded in Mt. Also suitable for Epiphany.

PREPARATION

Use an OHP with an overlay presentation that is developed in sequence. Ideas for the drawings can be obtained from looking at children's Bibles and books or at *Help, I Can't Draw!* books by Sheila Pigrem (Kingsway/Falcon). You want bold, clear, colourful pictures that are well drawn and hold people's attention on a familiar story. Use the star, text and headings either hinged on to the base frame on the outside of the overlap, or use them unhinged and independently, whichever works best for you.

Acetate 1

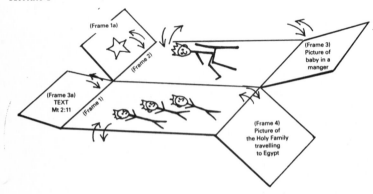

Prepare acetate 2 with the wording as indicated below.

PRESENTATION

Tell the story and develop your aim as you show each of the frames. Use a relaxed style and imaginatively fill out the story.

Acetate 1

Frame 1	The Wise Men follow the star (1a)
Frame 1 + 2	The Wise Men (minus star) meet with King Herod
Frame 1	The Wise Men follow the star
Frame 1 + 3	The Wise Men worship the new King
Frame 3a added	Text: Mt 2:11
Frame 2	King Herod's anger
Frame 2 + 4	The King in exile
	The escape of Jesus to Egypt.

Acetate 2 (headings only)

Wise Men—worship
Evil king—kills
King of Kings—loves.

What is our response to Jesus, the King of Love?

1 To lift him up in worship and praise?
2 To dash him down to reject and remove him?

Wise Men came to Jesus at the first Christmas. Wise men still do!

Ray Adams
Redditch

15 Jesus in the Temple as a Boy

TEXT

Lk 2:41–52. Special verse: Lk 2:51: 'His mother treasured all these things in her heart.' Other helpful verses that are a back-up to the theme of the talk: Eph 4:11–16; Col 1:3–14.

AIM

To show we need to follow the example of Jesus and grow up both spiritually and socially.

PREPARATION

You will require:

1 Photograph album
2 Eighteenth birthday card
3 Dress pattern.

PRESENTATION

1 *Show photograph album*
   Do any of you have family photograph albums at home? Most family photograph albums have various pictures of the family and children as they grow up. (Amplify, if helpful, with contributions from the congregation.) Our hearts and minds are rather like photograph albums; we store up pictures of the past and recall them by way of using our memories. Of course, in the days before photography, unless someone was very famous and had his picture painted or engraved, the only way to recall events of the past was by way of a good memory and then to have it written down. This explains our special verse of Lk 2:51. Mary, the mother of Jesus, had a good memory and, by retelling the story, passed on the event of the day they lost Jesus in Jerusalem, so that Luke was able to record it in his Good News about Jesus.

2   *Show eighteenth birthday card*

In our country today, when one is eighteen years old one is regarded as a man or woman; it used to be twenty-one years of age, and some people still keep that as a special day. (Amplify, if helpful with contributions from the congregation.) At eighteen years of age one can vote, should pay tax, and may fight for one's country. In fact, at eighteen years one has both civil rights and civil responsibilities that cover a wide range of one's life—one has grown up!

We need to prepare for this coming of age and to do so, we greatly benefit as Christians from our home, our school and our church. We need to grow up to be an adult by way of both a spiritual as well as a social development.

3   *Show a dress pattern*

A dress pattern provides a design that will enable us to make our clothes as intended. Has anyone made any mistakes by not following the pattern when clothes-making? (Draw out examples from the congregation.) Stick to the maker's instructions and the model's design, and all will be well. This is the point Luke is making in today's story.

Retell the story with an emphasis on the fact that Jesus was growing up both spiritually and socially.

(a)   *Jesus' visit to Jerusalem with his parents*

At twelve years of age, Jesus was preparing for his bar mitzvah. A Jewish boy becomes *bar mitzvah*, 'the son of the commandment', and assumes male adult responsibility before God for his actions when he reaches the age of twelve. Jesus was aware that he was growing up. Luke points out that Jesus' growth was both spiritual and social (v 52).

(b)   *Mary and Joseph lose Jesus at the great Passover festival*

Anyone who has had the experience of losing a child in a great crowd will know how they felt! This feast was one of the three major events that was centralised on Jerusalem each year. At this feast commemorating the rescue of the Israelites from Egypt, Jesus would be reminded of the character of God— God's grace and God's faithfulness.

71

(c) *Jesus talking to the Jewish teachers in the Temple courts*

In this great centre of worship, with its emphasis on the revealed Law of God and the nation's sacrifices to God, Jesus is found talking with growing spiritual understanding with the leading teachers of Judaism. The feast and the Temple would quite naturally draw them to discuss the character of God and our human relationship with God. It is here that Luke helps us to understand where spiritual growth comes from: knowing and doing God's will. Mary and Joseph learned that day that their son was growing up fast, growing spiritually and socially.

(d) *Jesus is reunited with his parents*

The obedience that Jesus showed to his human parents (v 51) is matched with his obedience to his heavenly Father. This whole occasion made a lasting impression upon Mary; it was now a treasured memory for her and for the early church. Luke uses this incident to teach us how we need to grow in a whole way, just as Jesus shows us (v 52).

Growing up affects all, young and old. We need continually to grow in maturity—a maturity that is spiritual and social. So let us remember that Jesus is our model, the Bible our guide and the Holy Spirit our helper.

Ray Adams
Redditch

16 Mothering Sunday: The Mother of Jesus

TEXT

Lk 1:38, 2:19, 51; Jn 2:5, 19:25–7; Acts 1:14.

AIM

To show forth Mary as a model mother.

PREPARATION

Prepare 7 transparencies as indicated below (or five, omitting nos 1 and 7).

PRESENTATION

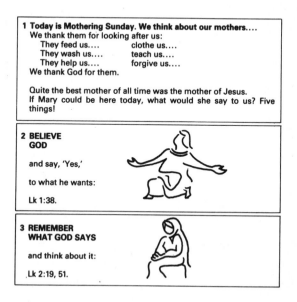

1 **Today is Mothering Sunday. We think about our mothers....**
We thank them for looking after us:

They feed us....	clothe us....
They wash us....	teach us....
They help us....	forgive us....

We thank God for them.

Quite the best mother of all time was the mother of Jesus.
If Mary could be here today, what would she say to us? Five things!

2 **BELIEVE GOD**

and say, 'Yes,'

to what he wants:

Lk 1:38.

3 **REMEMBER WHAT GOD SAYS**

and think about it:

Lk 2:19, 51.

4 DO WHATEVER JESUS TELLS YOU:

Jn 2:5.

5 RECEIVE JESUS' HELP:

Jn 19:25–27.

6 MEET TO PRAY AND WORSHIP WITH JESUS' FRIENDS:

Acts 1:14.

7 A FAITHFUL MOTHER:

Believes God
Remembers what God says
Encourages others to do what Jesus says
Receives Jesus' help
Meets to pray and worship with Jesus' friends.

Faithful sons and daughters copy her example.

Stewart Symons
Ardrossan and Irvine

17 Mothering Sunday: The Fifth Commandment

TEXT

Ex 20:12.

AIM

To encourage all ages to honour their parents.

PREPARATION

Have various sets of rules, eg *Highway Code*, rules for game. Four flash cards needed: 'T. Jones & Sons, Number 250' (or another appropriate name and house number); 'Obey'; 'Help'; 'Care'. You will also require various items of food, clothes, bib, feeding-bowl, spoon, money, clock, soap and towel, homework, television, two potato peelers, bowls and some potatoes, washing-line, pegs and washing, two sets of shopping.

PRESENTATION

Show *Highway Code* and rules for game and say there are also rules for a family. Quote Ex 20:12. Think of some of the benefits of being in family. Illustrate with visual aids.

Name (eg, 'T. Jones & Sons, Number 250'). Food is normally eaten with the family; home is where family live together; clothes are given to one by family—one isn't wearing any when born. Teaching (bib, feeding-bowl, spoon—you need to be sure you illustrate with something taught at home not school) is first done in the family. Money is earned by parents to buy things we need.

The commandment tells us to honour parents. Put up your three remaining flash cards as you reach each main point, showing how we do so.

Obey

(Col 3:20.) Areas where we need to do so are connected with: time (clock) we should be in or go to bed; cleanliness (soap and towel), when we want to do something else; homework, when we prefer not to get on with it; television—what and when we watch. Jesus obeyed his parents when twelve years old (Lk 2:51).

Help

Ask who can peel potatoes and start a potato-peeling competition. You will need someone to supervise while you carry on with the rest of your talk. Another way of helping is to hang out the washing. Have your line attached at one end and get a helper to fasten the other end. You can then time (in turn) two children hanging out the washing. Shopping, with the 'shop' at the back of church (with person in charge), can similarly be a race. Then see how your potato peelers are getting on. Prizes for the winners (from the shopping?) might be appropriate.

Care

Perhaps some of these things apply to adult members of congregation who still have parents alive. Get three members of congregation (from where they are—pre-arranged) to read the Bible verses. Mk 7:10–13. Explain 'corban'. Comments on 'doing things for the church' and neglecting parents. 1 Kings 2:19. Bathsheba was King Solomon's mother. Notice how he respected her. How do we respect our parents? 1 Tim 5:4 (be sensitive who you ask to read this). Talk about seeing parents and grandparents, phoning them or writing to them.

You could end with a brief comment about the promise of long life in the commandment, mentioning that in a family where children obey, help and care there is a happy and secure home. Summarise using flash cards.

(It may be possible to use parts of this talk to make a shorter talk, although the idea in some ways is to integrate activity into the talk itself, which allows the talk to be longer.)

Alan Pugmire
Manchester

18   The Triumphal Entry
(a crossword talk on Mt 21:1–13 NEB)

Jesus and his disciples came <u>14 across</u> (4) to Jerusalem. When they reached the Mount of <u>5 across</u> (6), Jesus sent two of the disciples on ahead with these instructions:

> You <u>13 across</u> (3) to <u>3 down</u> (2) to the village there ahead of you, and you will find straightaway a <u>2 down</u> (6) tied up. Untie it and bring it to me. If the person <u>1 across</u> (7) the donkey says anything, tell him, 'The Master needs it', and then he will let it go at once.

So the disciples went and did <u>19 across</u> (2) Jesus had told them to do; they brought the donkey, threw their cloaks over it and helped Jesus to <u>22 across</u> (3) on it. A large <u>1 down</u> (3) began to gather and they spread their coats on the road while others cut <u>7 across</u> (6) after <u>7 across</u> (6) from the trees to <u>28 across</u> (4) in their hands or <u>23 down</u> (2) spread them in the road. The crowds walking in front of Jesus and those walking behind began to <u>4 down</u> (4): '<u>9 down</u> (7) to <u>16 down</u> (6) Son! <u>11 across</u> (7) is <u>28 down</u> (2) who <u>26 across</u> (5) in the name of the <u>18 across</u> (4)! It was quite a <u>24 across</u> (5) procession. When Jesus <u>6 down</u> (7) through the <u>10 across</u> (4) of the city, there was uproar. Many <u>17 down</u> (6) <u>29 across</u> (7), 'Who is he?' Those who were <u>21 down</u> (4) to see him replied, 'This is the <u>25 down</u> (4) prophet Jesus from Nazareth.' Jesus <u>15 down</u> (4) through the city to the Temple, where he <u>20 across</u> (4) the whole crowd by causing all the traders to be <u>16 across</u> (6) out of the Temple. He overturned the tables of the money-changers and the stools of the <u>12 down</u> (7) in pigeons. Jesus said to them, 'It is written in the Scriptures that God said: "My Temple will be called a house of prayer"; how <u>27 across</u> (4) you make it a <u>8 down</u> (7) den?'

David McIntosh
Ellesmere Port

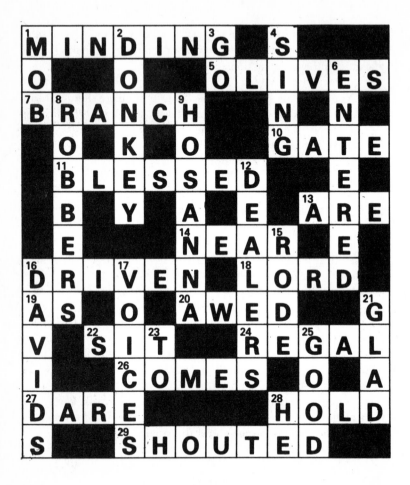

The Triumphal Entry (Mt 21:1–13 NEB)

19 Good Friday: No Separation from the Love of God

TEXT

Rom 8:31–9.

AIM

To acknowledge that we all need love and that perfect love is found in God alone.

PREPARATION

Either on teazlegraph or OHP acetates, prepare a wall as illustrated, where the cross in it is not evident until removed. On a large heart-shaped card (or acetate) print the word 'GOD'. On four circles a little smaller than the heart-shape, illustrate 'trials' (eg, a depressed-looking face), 'the future' (eg an H-bomb exploding), 'evil powers' (eg, a devil) and 'death' (eg, a tombstone).

PRESENTATION

If it is likely to be known, refer to the Beatles song 'All you need is love' and proceed to point out the universal need for love, with reference to children's need for parental love, etc. Perhaps mention that the hated Nazi propaganda minister, Dr Goebbels, could have been quite a different character if he had known love at home as a child.

Then state that most of all, we all need the love of God. Refer to the visual-aid board or OHP revealing the wall already in place and put 'GOD' on the far side of it.

Barriers to God's love

We often feel there are big barriers between us and God's love, such as (put up visuals on front side of wall as you refer to them):

1 *Trials*
   Paul faced many (v 35). Enlarge briefly on the sort of trials the congregation may have. Mention that some of these can come because we stand up for Jesus. We can feel very alone and God's love can seem far away.
2 *The future (v 38)*
   Mention the bomb, unemployment, illness, loneliness, etc. Can we be sure of God's provision and love?
3 *Evil powers (v 38)*
   Mention the dangers of the occult, with illustrations appropriate to the congregation, such as fascination with horoscopes and Ouija boards. Could we be separated from God's love?
4 *Death itself (v 38)*
   We know the Bible teaches God is love, but he is also holy. We are sinners (enlarge). How can we face God beyond death? Will we be separated from his love?

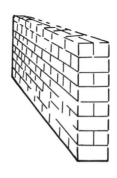

Nothing can separate us from the love of God

Refer to verses 37–9. How can we be so certain? (V 32.) Perhaps tell the story of Abraham's near sacrifice of his son Isaac. But God did not spare his own Son. What happened? Explain. Remove cross from the visual aid. If we have repented and believed, then we have nothing to fear. Whatever we feel, God's love is near. Mention Jesus' Resurrection, Ascension and intercession at the Father's side and quote verse 34, possibly adding Rom 5:1–2.

Michael Botting
Editor

20 Good Friday: Why Did God Allow It?

TEXT

Mt 27:46.

AIM

To explain why Jesus had to die and to attempt to give a reason why God does not intervene to prevent disasters. The talk could be used on Good Friday.

PREPARATION

Obtain a marionette, ie, a puppet worked by strings.

PRESENTATION

Begin by sympathising with your congregation about the problem of the terrible disasters that happen in the world, perhaps mentioning a recent one.

Introduce your marionette. Show how it jumps entirely to your tune as you pull its strings. Ask if it can love anyone? Hence explain how men and women have had to be given some real degree of free-will, which really means they can choose how they will behave. If they could not, then they would be no different from puppets on strings. Part of the story in Gen 2–3 could be mentioned.

Now if God always intervened every time we did something bad or stupid, we would simply become puppets. Sometimes people are very irresponsible. Men who run coal-mines are told that a coal tip is slipping and could engulf a school full of children. If they do nothing and it happens, as it did years ago in a Welsh mining village, who is to blame: God or the owners of the mine? However, we know God cares, because Jesus, his Son, came into the world, lived a perfect life, but eventually was taken prisoner, condemned to death because he claimed to be God (which was true), and was nailed to a cross to die. From that cross, Jesus cried, 'My God, my God, why have you forsaken me?' God the Father did not intervene even then, even though it was his own Son dying there in terrible agony. Why? For the same reason that he has given men freedom to behave in such a terrible way if they so choose. But also, in this case, because Jesus was dying as well for the sins of the world. That is how much God cares.

Let us always remember this when the next disaster strikes.

Michael Botting
Editor

21 Easter Day: The Emmaus Road

TEXT

Lk 24:13–35.

AIM

To encourage everyone to be open to God by meeting with the risen
Christ.

PREPARATION

Use an OHP.
   Prepare one of the following:

(a)   Four pictures revealed in sequence on one screen (as below).
      Use an acetate frame with four non-transparent windows that
      open up in sequence to reveal four pictures below on a separate
      acetate (see Talk 3).
(b)   Four pictures and words put separately on to the screen.
(c)   Draw figures as you tell the story—keep it simple, bold and
      colourful.

PRESENTATION

Open ears (v 27)

Tell the story of how, as they journeyed along the road to Emmaus,
Jesus drew near to the two travellers and opened their ears to the
teaching of scripture. (You could compare how all of us are journey-
ing on the road of life.)
   The Bible explains clearly why Jesus came to live as a servant on
earth, died sacrificially for the sin of all mankind and rose again as
the triumphant Saviour of the world. Jesus still speaks to us today
through the Bible. The message of the Bible is good news to those
who hear what it says and listen with open ears to the love story that

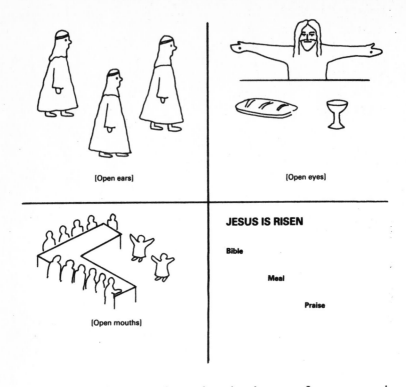

[Open ears]

[Open eyes]

[Open mouths]

JESUS IS RISEN

Bible

Meal

Praise

it has to tell. A love story that seeks to involve us, as Jesus communicates to us and journeys with us through life.

Open eyes (v 30)

When Jesus shared a meal with his two friends, he brought joy into their hearts and lives. Jesus gave himself to other people, especially at shared meals (compare with the feeding of the five thousand, the Last Supper). Here at Emmaus, Jesus opened the eyes of the two disciples to know and understand that the one who broke bread with them and drank wine together with them was their Leader, whose body was broken and blood shed for them. The Last Supper and the Lord's Supper are intertwined, so from this we see the importance of our Holy Communion service today. It should open our eyes to the risen Christ sharing himself with his friends. (Sing chorus 'Open our eyes, Lord, we want to see Jesus'.)

Open mouths (v 35)

Continue the story of how the two disciples returned to Jerusalem with joy, praising God and sharing their testimony with their friends: 'He's alive', 'He is risen', 'He is risen indeed', 'Alleluia'. Now as Christians, we have something to celebrate, to share and to proclaim. Don't be silent Christians—speak out and speak up for Jesus. He opened the mouths of the first Christians with loving boldness—follow their example. He brings us his peace (v 36).

Summary

Jesus is risen, and he meets with his followers today as he did with his two friends on the road to Emmaus.

Ray Adams
Redditch

22 Easter Day: Seed-time, Easter and Baptism

TEXT

Jn 12:24–5.

AIM

To use the fact of spring and seed-time to help illustrate truth relating to Easter and the Christian life, including baptism.

PREPARATION

Either have 3 large cards (perhaps 30″ x 20″ or 76 cm x 51 cm) that can be placed completely on to a teazlegraph board side by side, or make 3 acetates for an OHP. On to each card/acetate put the following:

Card/Acetate 1   Card/Acetate 2   Card/Acetate 3

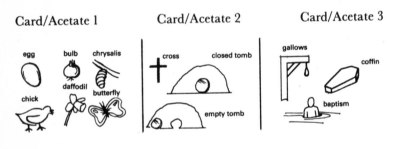

Have a small table lamp available plugged into an electric socket.

PRESENTATION

Pick up the table lamp and switch it on. Then remove the bulb and ask if any one will come up and put their fingers across the terminals inside the socket for a small prize. 'But surely if you are Christian, you will not be hurt?' Agree with the congregation that that will make no difference and that God works according to certain fixed laws! If we are so stupid as to touch electric terminals, we will get a nasty shock. From there, talk about another law of nature that we see all around us at this time of year:

New life

Bulbs planted in the ground a while ago are now producing beautiful daffodils. But other things seem to go through a sort of death before coming to new life, like eggs and chicks, chrysalises and butterflies. This is another law of nature: the way God works in his world. It was also true for:

Jesus

In the text Jesus is saying that, like a grain of wheat, he will have to go through a sort of death and coming to new life again. Put up second card or acetate and enlarge on the Easter story. But the same law is true for Christians in—

Baptism

Explain how we have to go through a kind of death to our old life if we are to be raised to new life. This symbolised by baptism (Rom 6:3f). Put up third card or acetate. But the same law is true for our everyday Christian life (v 25). Like John the Baptist, Jesus must increase in our lives, and we must decrease (Jn 3:30). Finally, at the end of our lives we have to go through death before we enter into the new life of heaven that God has prepared for us. Perhaps refer to the teaching of 1 Cor 15:35–6, 42–4 and to the resurrection body God has prepared for us who believe.

Conclude with the story of the American evangelist, D. L. Moody, who used to say that one day people would report that D. L. Moody was dead. 'Don't believe them, I shall be more alive than any one on earth.'

Michael Botting
Editor

23 Rogation: Looking After God's World

TEXT

Gen 2:15–23.

AIM

To encourage us all to look after God's world.

PREPARATION

1 Collect various objects that relate to each part of the talk. They
don't have to be the ones mentioned here as long as they are
appropriate, eg bits of rubbish, books on animals, bird nuts in a
string-bag.

2 Ask a member of the congregation if he or she would answer
some basic questions that express his or her interest in conservation. A young person in one of the uniformed organisations may
have a conservation badge. Some might belong to one of the
'Green' groups and, as Christians, might explain to everyone
why they are members.

PRESENTATION

Display title of talk

1 *Tidy the Earth*
(Display objects chosen, eg broken bottles, old fish-and-chip
paper, large oil-covered feather.) The Bible tells us (Gen 2:15)
that God wants us to work hard and take care of the world he
created (Gen 1:1). We don't own this world, but it is ours to look
after while we live here. Sadly, we often make a mess of our
towns and countryside, our hills, forests and oceans.

Here are some practical considerations:

(a) *Litter*. Don't drop it, use the litter-bins, take it away with you when you're on an outing, dump large unwanted objects at local council tips.

(b) *Pollution.* Remember the impact of air and water pollution, give support to our politicians to protect and preserve all things bright and beautiful. We can poison the atmosphere and rivers/seas causing great harm to the environment (ask for contemporary examples).

(c) *Waste land.* When we destroy the land and the forests, it is a loss to future generations and could endanger the whole Planet Earth. (Why not use recycled paper and help to protect our trees?)

2 *Protect the animals*

The Bible tells us (Gen 2:19–20) that man named the animals. In his floating zoo, Noah cared for the animals (Gen 7). Animals are part of the idyllic picture of peace that scripture paints for future humanity (Is 11). Here are some practical considerations:

(a) *Learn.* With the help of books, television, videos and talks, learn more about the animal world: where they live, what they eat, whether or not they are in immediate danger (compare them with the dodo). The animals' greatest danger comes from mankind—greedy and careless man. We should counter ignorance, indifference and illegal action.

(b) *Provide.* See to it that domestic animals are cared for. For wild animals in this country, let us make certain they are legally protected and these laws are upheld. Remember to feed the birds, don't disturb nests, close farm gates and generally be like Adam and Noah.

3 *Encourage other people*

The Bible shows how the people of God had to organise themselves, both morally and socially, after they came out of Egypt. Animals and the environment were part of that protection and preservation that came about under Moses. We still today need to have a shared concern for the world God has given us to live in. We need to understand, respect and provide for our environment (invite someone out to the front to be interviewed about their interest in conservation). Highlight these two areas, for example:

(a) *Organisations.* Mention local and national organisations that care for the countryside, animals, the world, etc.

(b) *Projects.* Many uniformed organisations have badges relating to conservation. Various schools, town councils and other groups seek to promote projects for tidying up the environment.

Conclusion

This is God's world—we don't own it, but we must look after it. God gave us a wonderful world; if it were much nearer the sun, it would be too hot to sustain life as we know it, and if it were much further from the sun, it would be too cold to provide for life as we know it. So be thankful and take care of God's world.

Ray Adams
Redditch

24 Jesus' Ascension

TEXT

Acts 1:6–11.

AIM

To consider what the Ascension meant to Jesus and what it should mean for us.

PREPARATION

An objects talk. The following objects are required:

1. An example of royal commemorative pottery (ie the Queen's Coronation mug, a plate from a royal wedding).
2. A picture of Jesus' Ascension (suggestions: a. La Rochette drawing; b. enlarged Annie Vallotton drawing from the Good News Bible. The Bible Society is very approachable about the use of the illustrations in the Good News Bible for services and small scale photocopying. A quick note or telephone call will usually bring permission—see page 275).

PRESENTATION

1. *Commemorative pottery object*
   Do you know what this is? (Show the example of commemorative pottery.)

   On important royal occasions such as coronations, weddings and anniversaries, we see in our shops a range of commemorative pottery for sale. Indeed, they have over the years become collectors' items. In the life of each king there are very important occasions that are remembered by the king's followers. For us, as Christians, we remember many things in the life of Jesus, the King of kings, and his final departure from earth, his Ascension, is one such important occasion. The story is recorded in the Bible in Lk 24 and Acts 1, and Luke, the author of both books, shows how Jesus' Ascension brings to an end his ministry on earth as the Gospels record it and opens up the life of the people of God in the life of the church as Acts describes it. The Ascension of Jesus is a pivot, a link of royal importance.

2 *Picture of Jesus' Ascension*
The importance of Jesus' Ascension lies not so much in how it happened, but why. The emphasis of the New Testament is that:

(a)   He is a High Priest who prays (intercedes) for us, so that we can worship God, even though he is completely pure and holy (Heb 4:14).

(b)   He is the Suffering Servant, who has both died and been raised to life again, showing that God is just *and* merciful and has made real salvation available for us all (Phil 2:9).

The importance of Jesus' Ascension applies to both Jesus and ourselves. Let us consider them.

3 *Jesus*
(a)   He completed the work for which he came to earth. Jesus defeated evil and sin; he brought God's forgiveness; he rescued us from slavery.

(b)   He provided a new opportunity for us to live in a right relationship with God. The gift of the Holy Spirit came from Jesus as the presence and power of God for the people of God.

In other words, Jesus' Ascension was an important royal occasion that was a turning-point for him and for us. The Ascension was not the end but rather the beginning of something new. It was both an ending and a beginning—like a wedding. One stage leads to another and finally he will return again. Here is, as the French say, *'Au revoir'*, not, 'Goodbye'.

4 *Ourselves*
Life does not stand still but goes on: time and events move. Life is very much a journey, and on the journey we commence and complete different activities in our lives:

In school life—each September we 'go up' to a new class or a

94

new school.

In family life—birthday parties mark occasions of 'growing up'. At death—various terms are used to describe going to heaven; 'passed on', 'gone before', 'promoted to glory'.

In all these events we use pictures or symbolic language to describe something that has finished and begun, something past and something new.

Jesus' Ascension is a reminder to us of important turning-points in life and that we should remember them and make the most of the life God has given us and the opportunities we have for a positive use of our lives. Our aim as Christians must surely be to look back with satisfaction and to look forward with hope in the way we make use of our daily lives. Make life worthwhile by living it for God. Sing 'Take my life and let it be'.

Ray Adams
Redditch

25 Whit Sunday: The Holy Spirit Is Not a Luxury

(The substance of this talk was provided by a sermon written by George H. Morrison, DD, published in *The Gateways of the Stars* [Hodder and Stoughton: London, 1927].)

TEXT

Lk 11:9–13; Mt 7:9; Jn 14:15–20.

AIM

To show that having the indwelling Holy Spirit in our lives is not an optional extra for the Christian, but an essential ingredient.

PREPARATION

You will need sets of four things (written on card or OHP) to illustrate 'Which is the odd one out?' eg: 'Matthew, Luke, John and Timothy'; 'apple, banana, potato and tomato'; 'fork, spoon, bowl and saucepan', etc. Also, on separate cards or acetate sheets, a picture of (1) a loaf of bread; (2) a fish; (3) an egg and (4) tongues of fire (or a dove) resting on a head.

PRESENTATION

Go through examples of 'odd one out' until (a) everybody has got the idea, or (b) those really keen to participate have had a chance, or (c) the children become restless! Then ask for the odd one out of bread, fish, egg and Holy Spirit (showing each in turn). All will probably agree that it is the latter. Then say that the Holy Spirit is really not the odd one out at all: it is in the same category as the other three. Ask for suggestions: all forms of food in some way? Not quite, but all are essential for life. Explain how bread, fish and eggs were the staple diet of the ordinary people of Jesus' day (explain 'staple', of course, if necessary). Meat was eaten only on special occasions, eg, weddings, Passover; and then often one lamb would be shared between many families.

We all need a basic diet to keep fit and healthy. (If time allows, elaborate on what is good and bad, essential or a luxury in our diet today.) So we all need the power of the Holy Spirit within us. Explain and elaborate on the things Jesus promised that the Holy Spirit would do. He is essential for a healthy spiritual life; just as children ask their parents for good food, as Christians we must ask God to give us his Holy Spirit—and he will.

David McIntosh
Ellesmere Port

26 The Fruit of the Spirit
(a crossword talk on Gal 5:22–3 GNB)

See page 31 for use of this talk.

ACROSS

1   Making again (12)
6   Disastrous (6)
8   Length of time (6)
9   See 20 down
11 Cease to live (3)
13 — (12)
15 Part of verb 'to be' (3)
16 Finishes (4,2)
18 Pair of people (5)
20 Long history (4)
21 — (8)
23 — (4)
24 — (3)
25 Remove, hat—for example

DOWN

1   Payment made by householders (5)
2   Terror (4)
3   — (6)
4   Single occasion (4)
5   — (8)
7   — (8)
8   — (8)
10 Mountain area near Gethsemane (6)
12 Fearful (6)
14 — (8)
17 — (5)
19 Choose (3)
20 And 9 across—(4–7)
22 Shake head (3)

David McIntosh
Ellesmere Port

1.R	E	2.F	A	3.S	H	I	4.O	N	I	N	G	5.G
A		E		P			N					O
6.T	R	A	G	I	C				7.K			O
E		R		R		8.P	E	R	I	O	D	D
S				I		R			N			N
	9.C	10.O	N	T	R	O	L		11.D	I	E	E
12.A		L				D			N			S
13.F	A	I	14.T	H	F	U	L	N	E	S	S	S
R		V	U		C			S				
15.A	R	E	M		16.E	N	D	S	U	P	17.P	
I		18.T	W	I	N	S					E	
D	19.O		L				20.S	A	G	A	A	
	21.P	A	T	I	22.E	N	C	E			C	
	T		T		O		23.L	O	V	E	E	
		24.J	O	Y		25.D	O	F	F			

The Fruit of the Spirit (Gal 5:22–3 GNB)

27 The Holiness and Majesty of God

TEXT

Is 6:1–8.

AIM

To show that the holiness and majesty of the Trinity make God a special Person to meet.

PREPARATION

Collect headlines and perhaps stories from the newspapers about the British royal family. Either write the headlines on card or on OHP acetates.

PRESENTATION

Using your visual aids, talk about the scramble for news about members of the royal family or the latest popular stars. Point out:

1 The importance of the photo opportunity to newsmen
2 How important to the media personal titbits seem to be—we feel we 'know' the royal family much better
3 Those who have met them feel special—and remember it
4 The intrusive nature of some reporting.

Now relate those four points to Persons of the Trinity, a Royal Family of three Persons:

Jesus: So much more than a brief photo opportunity; he laid aside his majesty to live God's love among us for over thirty years.

The Holy Spirit: More than a brief meeting with royalty; he comes to live in us, knowing us better than we know ourselves.

The Father: Rightly, there is always an 'otherness' which leads to respect. As with earthly royalty, we feel attracted and want to know more, which is not surprising, considering we are made in God's image.

Just as the media scramble after news of royalty, but would much prefer to meet them in person, so we can scramble to know more about God, say, from the Bible; but even that is not the same as meeting him in person. In fact, for all his holiness and majesty, God longs to meet with us, because we are already special to him. We don't have to be worthy of a medal to meet God! He makes us worthy as he did with Isaiah (explain about the text).

God's majesty and holiness are so great that we will never fully understand him. We should not fear being intrusive, as the media sometimes are with royalty: we already have an invitation to meet with God.

Robert Cadman
Chelmsford

28 Trinity Sunday: The Trinity and Stability

TEXT

Mal 3:6a (GNB); Is 6:1–8.

AIM

To teach something about the stability of God and its implications—in a simple way.

PREPARATION

Obtain five pieces of wood with holes at each end, and four nuts and bolts to fasten them together. Two pieces should be 3' or 0.9m, two pieces 4' or 1.2m, and one piece 5' or 1.5m in length (or multiples thereof).

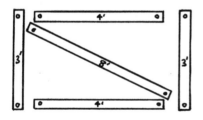 

Dismantle a three-legged stool, or make one with legs you can detach.

Alternatively, prepare appropriate transparencies for OHP to illustrate the same points.

PRESENTATION

'I am the Lord, and I do not change' (Mal 3:6). There is stability with God.

Take a three-legged stool. There is stability only when all three legs are in place. (Demonstrate with just one..., two, etc.)

'Ah!' you might say, 'What about four legs?' Actually, four legs are less stable. One needs equal legs and a flat floor or one wobbles. For uneven ground and all conditions, it is three legs one needs— like artists' easels and photographers' tripods.

The engineer building bridges and the architect designing roofs both know a similar thing. It is a triangular structure that is stable. (Demonstrate with the two 3' and two 4' pieces bolted together into a rectangle and show how it can be pushed sideways, then bolt the 5' piece diagonally. It is now stable, being two triangles. You can then take one 3' and one 4' piece off, still leaving them bolted where they join, to emphasise the point.)

So it should not surprise us to learn that God is threesome, that he is a Trinity, and that his threesomeness means his stability. It means he 'is the same yesterday and today and for ever' (Heb 13:8). It means he does not change. He is reliable, faithful, doesn't let one down. He keeps his word—his promises and threats. You can rest on him, he supports—no strain of self-balancing required.

I want to close by emphasising two things:

1 He keeps his word: his promises and his threats. The historical record of both the Bible and the church down to this day proves just this.
2 We need therefore, to take his threats seriously, and his promises seriously. We need to: repent and seek forgiveness for sin (Holy, holy, holy.); believe and put our faith in Jesus (hot coal = application of the sacrifice); obey and give him first place in our lives (here am I. Send me.).

NB: The final allusions in brackets are with reference to Isaiah 6, one of the traditional readings for Trinity Sunday. If this passage has been read, an aside to any adults present, linking the talk to the Isaiah reading may be appreciated.

Stewart Symons
Ardrossan and Irvine

29 Sea Sunday

TEXT

Jn 21:1–14.

AIM

To 'see' Jesus.

PREPARATION

Prepare three acetate sheets (A, B, C). B should be a clear acetate sheet with a piece of paper stuck over it, a shape of a fish having been cut out. The three sheets are then joined together on the same side. Sheet A should be attached to the cardboard border, next comes C and finally B (see fig 1).

Secondly, a scene should be prepared with the fishermen (fig 2). To be used with this acetate, you need to prepare at least thirty small fish shapes from paper.

Prepare an acetate showing Jesus by a fire on the shore. To overlay this one, a scene with the fish being handed over to Jesus (fig 3).

Lastly, prepare an acetate with the words 'SEA' and 'SEE' (fig 4). Masked under two separate flaps of paper, write the rest of the words seen in the diagram.

PRESENTATION

Quite simply, retell the story. Use the acetates as shown in fig 1. The disciples are out at sea. Question: 'Why?' and 'What' are they doing? Flap over B and C together.

At this point you can talk about food provided for us by those at sea. This gives room to talk a little about Sea Sunday. Food is provided for our bodies, so we can grow up. Perhaps you could ask about the fish-eating habits of the congregation. Use the top part of the SEA-SEE acetate (fig 4).

Out at sea

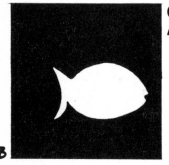

Q: What are they doing?
A: Catching fish

Food for bodies
...to grow up

Q: Whom did they see?
A: Jesus

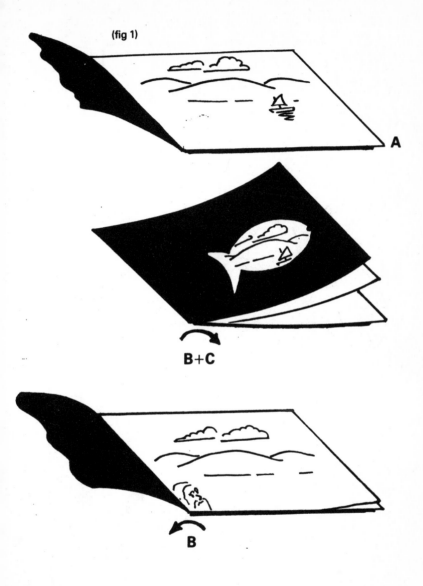

(fig 2)

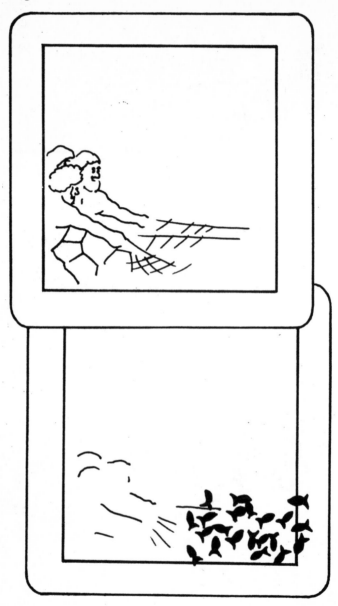

(fig 3)

(fig 4)

Going back to the disciples—they saw little reward for their efforts, they had been going all night. But they did see someone else. (Fold back B to reveal Jesus.) Question: Whom did they see?

Re-enact the conversation at this point. (Project fig 2.) Ask a youngster to come and place some fish on the screen. Build it up a little: Did they catch one? Did they catch two, three...ten? How many? (Put on a few more each time, but not the full number or you will obscure the whole screen!)

Now change to the picture of Jesus on the shore (fig 3). Jesus could have provided all they needed (remember the boy with the fish and bread). However, just like at that time, he wanted people to be involved. Question: Why? So that they could see (fig 4). Tickle out the two meanings of the word 'see' (literally, seeing before our eyes, and seeing with understanding). They could see Jesus and all he could do. He gave them food for faith, to help them to grow up in their faith. Go back to the text to explain this idea.

God could give us all the food we need, eg, from the sea. He wants us to work for it, so we see his creation. He could give us all the faith we need, but we grow by seeing and understanding God at work.

Graeme Skinner
Bebington

30 The Transfiguration

Mt 17:1–13; Mk 9:2–13; Lk 9:28–36.

AIM

To tell the story of the Transfiguration, and draw some implications.

PREPARATION

Use masking tape to connect four acetates together as shown. Note that it is often a good idea to shave an edge off acetates that fold in; this should stop the buckling effect.

Draw a picture of Jesus on the central acetate. Fold over the left acetate and blank out all of the area around the figure. (This is best done with paper stuck on to the surface of the acetate.) While the left is still folded over, colour in the appropriate areas: yellow skin and blue stripes.

Fold the left side away, and fold over the right side. Then draw two figures either side of Jesus. Fold this one away and fold down the top acetate. A cloud effect can be made for this picture. Letraset shading is expensive, and a good effect can be obtained by drawing. Better still, if your photocopier takes duplicating acetates, photocopy a black page. This can then be cut as shown and stuck on the picture to form acetate 1.

PRESENTATION

Basically, the slide can be used for telling the story of the Transfiguration. The raising and lowering of the flaps enhance the reading of the text. Start with the masked-out left side over the picture of Jesus. When the left is lifted off (1), then Jesus shines, as he is that much brighter. Fold in the right side (2), and the two appear with Jesus. Finally, fold down (3) and the figures are partly hidden by a cloud.

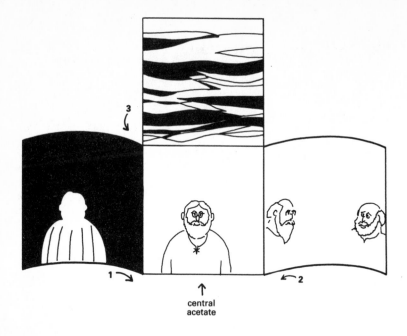

central
acetate

At this point, for a dramatic effect, use a loudhailer or the PA system to broadcast God's voice. Can the congregation think of other times God spoke about Jesus? Can people think of other times there were clouds associated with Jesus? What was said? What does this tell us about Jesus?

Notice the disciples' reaction. What's our reaction? This is the sort of story when it might be possible to 'interview' some of the children out front. Either ask them beforehand to be Peter, James and John; or ask them what they learn about Jesus from the story.

Graeme Skinner
Bebington

31 Harvest

TEXT

Mt 13:24–30.

AIM

To warn about judgement and teach how we may be accepted by God.

PREPARATION

You will require a teazlegraph board and figures with Velcro backing.

Make six dark-green cardboard figures.
Secured with two winged paper-clips.

Stick light-green or yellow paper on the back of two of them.
These two need Velcro on both sides and a fluffy piece of Velcro in the centre on the yellow side.
Make two small crosses of red card with Velcro on back (these should fit the figures—see below) and some flames, as shown below.
You will also need two pieces of card to represent the barn (as shown below).

113

Prepare six coloured flower heads to fit on dark-green figures.

PRESENTATION

Talk about farming or gardening, sowing seeds and harvesting. What does the gardener do with the weeds? At harvest we bring good things not weeds.

Tell the parable. At the harvest what did the farmer do with the: (a) corn; (b) weeds? Did he want the weeds in his barn?

(Uncover board with all dark-green sides showing.) Which are the good plants? Which are the weeds?

However, Jesus was not talking about plants but people. (Remove heads and turn down leaves.)

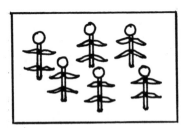

Jesus was talking about those fit to enter God's kingdom and those only fit to be thrown out like rubbish, which is very serious. Because God loves everyone, he wants everyone included, so he gives this warning.

Heaven is a perfect place, no sadness, cruelty, etc—so only perfect people there! But no one is perfect! The good news of Jesus is REPENT, means turn around (reverse two figures to show yellow side) and BELIEVE (add crosses to these two); then we are forgiven and fit for God.

On earth we all live together and it is not easy to tell who has turned and trusted Jesus, but at God's harvest those who have accepted Jesus and been forgiven will be with God. Those who have not will be like the weeds; we don't know just what this means except that they are NOT with God. (Rearrange the board as shown.) Jesus invites us to believe and warns of the consequences of not doing so.

We have brought good things, not rubbish, to harvest thanksgiving. We offer ourselves to God by repenting and believing. At harvest we thank God for the good things of life and for the good news of Jesus, so that we can live with God in his kingdom.

Judith Rose
Gillingham, Kent

32   Harvest: A Tale of Two Oranges

TEXT

Mk 8:35 and/or Jn 12:24, with Mk 6:30–44 as the reading.

AIM

To teach that we must be 'broken' to be useful.

PREPARATION

Prepare eight transparencies with suitable use of colour—orange for
outline of oranges and facial features, green stalks, brown branches,
blue lettering at top, black lettering below, etc—as shown below.

PRESENTATION

Think about the whole subject beforehand, and then use the transparencies as the notes for your talk. At harvest-time you may wish to
start with reference to all the produce which has been brought and
then pick out two oranges and go on from there. 'Today I want to
tell you the tale of two oranges. It is a kind of parable... I am going
to call one 'Bubble' and the other 'Squeak', and you'll find out why
as we proceed.... In the beginning they both grew round and ripe,
and they both enjoyed the sun and praising God....'

After transparency 2 and before 3, you will need to say something
about Bubble being full of Sonshine joy—adventurous, responsive
to God's purposes and Spirit—while Squeak is full of fear, wanting
not to be disturbed, afraid of change.

After transparency 7, you may wish to add, Squeak ends up with
no appeal [deliberately saying it as 'no uh peel'!], and all because he
did not want to be disturbed.

While talking about transparency 8, if you have used Mk 6, you
may wish to draw attention to the fact that the bread when broken
by Jesus was then used to feed thousands.

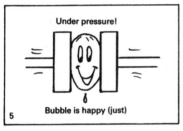

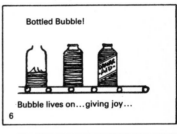

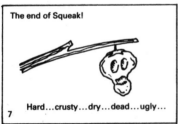

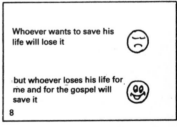

Stewart Symons
Ardrossan and Irvine

Barry Lomax
Wimborne

33   Fireworks: A Talk for Early November

TEXT

Lk 24:49; Rom 1:16; 1 Cor 1:18.

AIM

To show that we need to be active, dynamic Christians.

PREPARATION

You will need a selection of fireworks, as the headings suggest. You could use spent ones (if they are still recognisable), new ones (taking great care and pointing this out—watch proximity to candles, especially!) or larger dummies made from kitchen-roll tubes, etc, this being the best option! These need to be in a 'selection box'.

PRESENTATION

Talk a little about the fun of Bonfire night, and the variety of fireworks available, and lead on to how churchpeople can come in quite a variety, too. Open your box, and produce the following in turn:

Snowstorm

Establish that this throws white sparks everywhere, covering the ground, just like a real snowstorm. Everything is covered and looks the same until the snow melts/firework is over, when the real state of the ground is there for all to see. There are people like this, who look good on the outside, but are very different on the inside. Jesus said that it is what is on the inside that really matters.

Traffic-lights

Establish that this changes colour from red to amber to green, etc, just like the lights we see on the road—and we all know what it's like to be caught in a succession of lights: stop-go-stop-go. There are people like this, too, who are sometimes enthusiastic and keen, and at other times cold and uninterested. They come every week for a while, and then we do not see them for months.

Vesuvius/volcano

Establish that this erupts every now and again, and is quiet in between, just like a real volcano, which looks like an ordinary mountain, and just when least expected, there is a great explosion with molten rock everywhere. There are also people like this, who come every week, sit quietly, and go away until next week. They say or do little, but are always there. Then when it is least expected (and often when you change something), they erupt in protest, only to settle down until the next time.

Catherine-wheel

Establish that this goes round in circles, sends out lots of sparks, but ends up in the same place at the end. People like this are the ones who are always busy, rushing round in a panic, and visible to everyone. The problem is they just go round in circles and never really get anywhere.

Rocket

Establish that this is very dramatic as it shoots up into the air, is seen by many people, and then dies and falls to the ground. It is spectacular; it may be seen for several miles—but it does not last. There are people like this, who make a very public and spectacular commitment to Jesus, over whom a great fuss is often made, but who then drop away quickly.

Banger

You may think this is just a big noise which is all over in seconds, but the banger's big brother is more than just a noise. Dynamite is used in quarrying and mining, tunnelling and demolition. It is a very important and useful tool in the right hands.

The word 'dynamite' is from the Greek word *'dunamis'*, which means 'power', and that is what God gives us and wants us to allow him to use.

The promised power of the Holy spirit is dynamite, and the

power of the gospel is dynamite—the same word is used for both. God is calling us to be dynamite Christians, open to his power, and willing to serve him.

Which sort are you? Snowstorm, traffic-lights, volcano, Catherine-wheel, rocket or dynamite?

Note

These points could all bear further examination and explanation. Why are some churchpeople like this? This is really beyond the scope of this talk (and perhaps of a family service), but there could be a sermon series here.

Ian J Hutchings
Partington, Manchester

34 Bonfire Celebrations

Gen 22; Ex 3; 1 Kings 18; Dan 3.

AIM

To show four Bible bonfires and briefly comment on how in each of them God's servants were thankful to God.

PREPARATION

Use an OHP. You will need either (a) four pictures and words revealed in sequence on one screen (use an acetate frame with four non-transparent windows that can be opened up when required [see Talk 3]), or (b) four pictures and words put separately on to screen. The four pictures can be magnified/traced from the pictures of Annie Vallotton as used in the Good News Bible (see note on page 93).

1) The Lord provides (Pic from GNB) God's sacrifice	2) The Lord plans (Pic from GNB) God's guidance
3) The Lord presides (Pic from GNB) God's power	4) The Lord protects (Pic from GNB) God's presence

PRESENTATION

Bonfires

Originally they were called 'bone fires'. In Europe, animals were slaughtered before winter if they were not to be kept, sheltered and fed over winter. The meat of the animals was kept and the bones and carcasses burnt, hence the words 'bone fires'. The hilltop bonfire has been used as a means of communication: it was used as a warning signal (eg, bonfires warned of the approaching Spanish Armada of 1588). Bonfires have also been associated with times of celebration and thanksgiving. The bonfire celebrations of 5th November arose from the annual thanksgiving for the deliverance of king and government from the Gunpowder Plot. It was at one time a solemn day of observance in the Anglican *Book of Common Prayer*.

Bible bonfires

1 *The story of Abraham and Isaac (Gen 22)*
   Briefly retell the story, emphasising: (a) the Lord provides; (b) God's sacrifice.
2 *The story of Moses and the burning bush (Ex 3)*
   Briefly retell the story, emphasising: (a) the Lord plans; (b) God's guidance.
3 *The story of Elijah on Mount Carmel (1 Kings 18)*
   Briefly retell the story, emphasising: (a) the Lord presides; (b) God's power.
4 *The story of Daniel's three friends in the furnace (Dan 3)*
   Briefly retell the story, emphasising: (a) the Lord protects; (b) God's presence.

Conclusion

The bonfire celebrations of 5th November point to an important and significant event of history. Bible bonfires do the same. They point to a living God who cares and acts, who revealed himself to his servants of Bible days. We continue to worship and celebrate the same living God today, who by his Holy Spirit lights a fire in our hearts that we should never put out (1 Thess 5:19).

Ray Adams
Redditch

35 Guy Fawkes—Confession and Forgiveness

TEXT

Is 59:1–20.

AIM

To show that sin which is confessed is completely forgiven.

PREPARATION

For this talk, you will need to obtain or make:

1 A guy
2 Pictures of St Michael le Belfrey, York Minster, and Houses of Parliament
3 Cardboard boxes with following words on sides: 'lies'; 'hurt others'; 'evil plots'; 'murder'; 'ruin and destruction'; 'no one safe'
4 Box of matches
5 Ash from previously burnt newspaper (in a tin).

PRESENTATION

Say you have brought someone with you and produce your guy. Explain he was a real person, baptised at St Michael le Belfrey, York, next to York Minster (picture) who became a Roman Catholic. Famous because he tried to blow up Houses of Parliament. Caught and executed. Therefore, though he was baptised, religious and clever, he wasted his life. Many people who are baptised, religious and clever waste their lives. Are you going to be like that?

What did he do? Things similar to those condemned by Isaiah hundreds of years before him. Work through Is 59:1–8 and for each point, produce a box with label and after explaining how Guy Fawkes did these things, how they happen today, perhaps using recent incidents, and how we can do them, throw box on to a heap in the middle of the floor. Points are *lies* (vv 3–4), plans to *hurt others* (v 4), *evil plots* (vv 5–6), *murder* (v 7), *ruin and destruction* (v 7) and *no one safe* (v 8). People waste their lives by doing these things, even though they may be baptised, religious or clever.

Guy Fawkes didn't admit he was wrong and change his ways. Many don't today. But people in Isaiah's day did (vv 12–13). They were saying that they wanted to get rid of rubbish in their lives. What happens to rubbish at this time of year? Bonfire. Put guy on bonfire and produce your matches! (Don't light the bonfire, and make sure you put matches well out of the way, for after the service). Explain that telling God about wrong things in our lives is like saying they are rubbish we want to get rid of. We sometimes call this action 'confession'.

What happens to burnt newspaper? Becomes ash. (Produce your tin with ash in it.) You can't read it. God says he will 'save all of you that turn from your sins' (v 20 GNB). The sins will be completely gone. That is what it means to receive God's forgiveness.

We may not be like Guy Fawkes and try to blow up the Houses of Parliament, but we do wrong things. If there is no confession, there is no forgiveness, and we too will have wasted lives.

Alan Pugmire
Manchester

36 Poppy: Remembrance Day (1)

TEXT

Heb 9:22 (GNB).

AIM

To use the symbol of the poppy to speak of sin, blood and new life.

PREPARATION

Make a large poppy in coloured card, using winged paper-clips to hold the parts together.

PRESENTATION

(Appear with the large cut-out poppy—how will depend upon local set-up, but it is suggested you might withdraw to a vestry and then re-emerge wearing this over-size poppy—this immediately focuses attention.)

The poppy is an emblem of remembrance. It dates back to the end of the First World War, the Great War of 1914–18. The battles of those years were from trenches, and row upon row of men fell and died in the fields of Flanders, fields where blood-red poppies grew. So we wear poppies in remembrance of the men who died then and who have died since for our country.

Let's take a closer look at my poppy. (Proceed to dismantle into its three parts, and hold up each part as you speak.)

1 *My poppy reminds me of SIN—something BLACK*
It is a sad fact of history that sin causes bloodshed; and that bloodshed is the only way to bring a halt to sin. So men have fought and died to defend good and destroy tyranny. Always there was the hope that the war fought at the time would be the war to end wars—but it has not proved so in the past, and it is

still with us today in an awkward way in Northern Ireland. We still need armies.

2   *My poppy reminds me of BLOOD—something RED*
'Sins are forgiven only if blood is poured out' (Heb 9:22).

The sin of bloodshed can be controlled to some extent through the means of law and order, and armed force. It is important and fully recognised in the Bible and in the teaching of our Lord. It is wrong to deny or belittle it. Nevertheless, the Christian must always point to the deeper truths and to the permanent solution to sin in the hearts of men and of ourselves. It is out of the heart of man that proceeds sin which unchecked leads to murder, adultery, violence, corruption. If, to control sin blood sometimes needs to be shed, to cure sin Jesus' blood had to be shed.

3   *My poppy reminds me of NEW LIFE—something GREEN*
After wars are lost and won comes the task of building up, starting afresh to build a new life. The key to real new life in the hearts of men is that they acknowledge their sin and turn to Jesus for forgiveness—so that their sins may be cleansed in his blood—and then they will have new life. Truly ask Jesus into your life and he brings with his Spirit, as he enters your heart, new life.

Stewart Symons
Irvine and Ardrossan

37 Last Supper: Remembrance Day (2)

TEXT

1 Cor 11:24–56.

AIM

To contrast the symbols of bread and wine with the symbol of a poppy in the exercise of remembrance.

PREPARATION

Make a large poppy in coloured card. Have a loaf of bread and a bottle of wine to hand.

PRESENTATION

Assuming this talk is given on Remembrance Sunday, refer to the day and ask how we remember. Explain how the First World War was chiefly fought from trenches. Men would try to run to enemy trenches, get mown down by machine-gun fire and lie dead in fields of Flanders poppies. To help us remember, poppies have been sold since 1921, a sale which also raises money for those still suffering as a result of other wars.

Ask if anyone can think of another important event that we remember by means of a special visual aid. Lead into talk about the Last Supper and produce the bread and wine.

The Last Supper

Jesus said, 'Do this *in remembrance* of me' (v 24).

The apostle Paul wrote: 'You proclaim the Lord's death until he comes' (v 26).

However, there was a very big difference between the death of the men in Flanders, that we remember with the poppy, and the death of Jesus, that we remember with bread and wine:

1   (a)   *Man has to die some time*

We are all sinners and 'the wages of sin is death' (Rom 6:23), so our lives are already forfeit. Our lives, though our most precious possession, are no more valuable than anyone else's.

(b)   *Jesus never had to die*

Enlarge on his sinlessness. His life was of infinite value. When he died, none other than the life of the Son of God was being sacrificed.

2   (a)   *Man did not give his life voluntarily*

Though there were remarkable and noble acts of bravery, all attempted to avoid death if at all possible.

(b)   *Jesus gave his life voluntarily*

Quote Jn 10:18. Refer to the struggle in the Garden of Gethsemane and Jesus' words to Pilate (Jn 19:11). On the cross, Jesus commended his spirit into the hands of God and died. He was not dying for his own sins, for he had none, but for ours. His subsequent Resurrection is proof of this.

3   (a)   *Man would not die for his enemies*

In war men are prepared to give their lives for their friends. As Jesus said, there is no greater love we can show than to do so (Jn 15:13). But Jesus went further.

(b)   *Jesus died for his enemies*

Quote Rom 5:6–8, 10. He did not die for us because we are lovely, because, as sinners, we are not. He died for us because he is love. The cross shows how much he loved. There he died for us the ungodly. Why?

4   (a)   *Man only won for us a temporary extension of life*

If the Lord tarries, we shall all die eventually. After the First World War, there was a peace of only twenty years.

(b)   *Jesus won for us eternal life*

Quote Jn 3:16, 10:10b. Jesus did something for us that we could not do for ourselves. That is why he took bread and wine for us to remember it. That is why we must proclaim it, that all may know.

Because we should be grateful for what men have done for us in the wars, we should want to buy a poppy. But how much more should we want to respond to Jesus, not just by giving him our pennies and pounds, but by giving him our lives, that we might have the eternal life he won for us by his death.

Michael Botting
Editor
Stewart Symons
Ardrossan and Irvine

38 Christian Unity Week

TEXT

Jn 3:16; Eph 4:5.

AIM

To relate the love of Christianity to the life of Christ's church.

PREPARATION

Use an OHP or magnetic board with drawings.

For the OHP presentation, you will require either (a) four pictures and words revealed in sequence on one screen, as below (use an acetate frame with four non-transparent windows that open up in sequence to reveal four pictures below on a separate acetate frame [see Talk 3]), or (b) four pictures and words put separately on to the screen.

PRESENTATION

1 Jn 3:16. (Show picture of world with gold light around it.) Our life comes from the love of God (this thought can be expanded as required).
2 Eph 4:5. (Show picture of one-way traffic sign.) The church of Jesus Christ is united by God in love and life. The 'one holy catholic and apostolic church', as the Nicene Creed declares, is *one* in itself and for God alone. 'Lord': Jesus is Lord of all, loves all, life of all. 'Faith': the good news is to be shared by all Christians. 'Baptism': we belong to a worldwide fellowship.
3 This sign shows both converging and separating roads. The church is made up of many different Christian groups. The *many* are part of the *one*. Many different countries, cultures and convictions combine to make the church of Christ. Let us rejoice in our differences as long as we seek to contribute to the completeness of

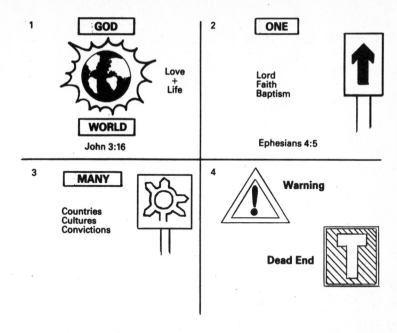

the united church. However, we should always work for a harmony of relationships that binds us together. We can also compare the different denominations to the different colours of the single rainbow, the different instruments of the single orchestra, and register how in each illustration they work together to bring harmony and unity.

4 The warning sign and dead-end sign remind us that, even with the one church with its many parts, we need to be aware of heresy as a denial of the faith we hold together, and of the cults as a denial of the love we hold together. Those who destroy the basis of faith and those who declare that they alone are the true church are both working against the teaching of Jn 3:16 and Eph 4:5. (Remember what Jesus said about the broad and narrow roads in Mt 7:13–14.)

Conclusion

The Christian faith and the Christian church are interrelated. When the faith is promoted, the church is protected. The love of God and the life of God go together in the unity of God's church. Writing to the early Christians, John the Elder sought to help them to understand this.

The first letter of John provides a spiral of themes concerning light, life and love. Here is the answer John gives that expresses basic Christianity for the united fellowship of the Christian church. Let us hold on to it!

Ray Adams
Redditch

39 One World Week: All One in Christ Jesus (late October)

Gal 3:28 (GNB); Mt 25:31–46; Eph 2:14.

AIM

To emphasise that whatever our nationality, race or colour we are all part of God's family, and that, as Christians, we must live so as to show that God's love extends to all.

PREPARATION

Ask a friendly travel agent for posters of people and places from North, South, East and West (eg, Eskimos/Canada; Aborigines/ Australia; people of India or Japan; Europe). Also required are a picture of a Russian church or Orthodox priest; Christian Aid poster of needy Third World. Include the singing of 'When I needed a neighbour' in the service.

PRESENTATION

Show travel posters and ask for identification and comment. Remind listeners of the fact that the family of the church is worldwide. Quote Gal 3:28: 'So there is no difference between Jews and Gentiles, between slaves and free men, between men and women; you are all one in union with Christ Jesus.' Comment that we are all a mixture because of the spread of Christianity; that language is not a barrier between Christians—this may be illustrated by an incident related by Brother Andrew in his book *God's Smuggler* (Hodder & Stoughton, 1968).

He arrived late one Saturday night in a place called Cluj in Romania and the next morning asked the hotel receptionist where he could find a church. The clerk looked at him suspiciously and told him, 'We don't have many of those, and in any case you wouldn't understand the language.'

'That's OK,' said Brother Andrew, 'Christians speak a kind of universal language.'

'What's that?' said the clerk.

'*Agapé*'.

'Never heard of it,' replied the clerk.

'Pity, it's the most beautiful language in the world.'

The following Sunday, Brother Andrew met the president of a Protestant church in his social headquarters and was frustrated to find that neither he nor the secretary spoke a word of Andrew's languages, nor he theirs. Then Andrew saw that the president had a well-worn Romanian Bible on his desk, so he took out his own Dutch Bible and turned to 1 Cor 16:20: 'All the brothers here send you greetings. Greet one another with a holy kiss.' He held out his Bible so that they could see the name of the book—recognisable in any language—and pointed out the chapter and verse. Their faces lit up as they found the same verse in the Romanian Bible and read it.

Then the President thumbed through his Bible until he found Prov 25:25: 'Like cold water to a weary soul is good news from a distant land.' For half an hour they continued, laughing with tears of joy in their eyes as they searched for just the verses they needed.

That evening, as Andrew entered the hotel, the receptionist stopped him. 'Say,' he said, 'I looked up that "*agapé*" in the dictionary. There's no language by that name. It's just a Greek word for love.'

'Quite so,' said Brother Andrew, 'I was speaking in it all afternoon.' (This story would adapt very easily and effectively as a sketch.)

Show picture of Orthodox priest (or Russian church). There are millions of Christians in the Soviet Union; we are sometimes encouraged by politicians and generals to think of Russians as potential, if not actual, enemies; but they are our brothers and sisters in Christ before all else, and that fact must govern our attitude to them. Ask what other countries are thought of as enemies by many in the West though in fact most of the people there are Christians.

If you wish, tell the story of the peace treaty between Argentina and Chile (related in *Marching Orders* by William Barclay, Hodder & Stoughton, 1973, pp 135–6).

There's never been a war between Argentina and Chile, but in 1899 the two countries were poised to begin hostilities over a border dispute, and by Easter 1900 war seemed inevitable. However, an Argentine bishop (Monsignor Benavente) preached an Easter Day sermon in Buenos Aires that was a passionate plea for peace, and news of this appeal was carried to Chile, where a Chilean bishop took up the message. Both bishops then set out on a campaign for peace in their respective countries. At first not much seemed to happen, but eventually public opinion forced the two governments to negotiate, and King Edward VII was called to arbitrate. A treaty was signed and a wonderful thing happened: the guns of the frontier fortresses, now useless and irrelevant, were melted down and made into a great bronze figure of Jesus, which was hauled 13,000 ft up to the frontier. Beneath it are the words: 'These mountains themselves shall fall and crumble to dust before the people of Chile and the Argentine Republic forget their solemn covenant sworn at the feet of Christ.' On the other side is the text (Eph 2:14 AV): 'He is our peace, who hath made both one.'

God intends *all* nations to be friends: Christians must be first to see that all should, and can, live in peace in the world.

Show pictures of Third World. These are our brothers and sisters too. How do we react to such pictures as these? Listen to what James says:

> Suppose there are brothers and sisters who need clothes and don't have enough to eat. What good is there in your saying to them, 'God bless you! Keep warm and eat well'—if you don't give them the necessities of life? So it is with faith: if it is alone and includes no actions, then it is dead (Jas 2:15–17 GNB).

Jesus told the story of the Good Samaritan to show that anyone in need is our neighbour (retell here, if time permits). We have sung (will shortly sing) 'When I needed a neighbour'; one day we shall all stand before Jesus and he will judge us as he says in Mt 25:31–46 ('I tell you, whenever you refused to help one of these least important ones, you refused to help me' v 45 GNB). We all belong to one world and everyone, good or bad, lovely or horrible, rich or poor, is our brother or sister. Christians must be the first to show how this can be true through the love of Christ, because we believe he died to save the whole world.

David McIntosh
Ellesmere Port

40 Speed the Plough! A Talk for Plough Sunday (January)

TEXT

Lk 12:16–21.

AIM

To encourage thankfulness for our daily food and those who work for it (at an unlikely time of the year).

PREPARATION

All you need is a plough in church! The simple garden wheel-hoe with a plough attachment is ample if you can find one, or you might have a local farmer who has a small plough you could borrow. If all else fails, have a suitable picture! Have your musician(s), ready to play a few bars of 'We Plough the Fields' too!

PRESENTATION

What's this music? (Ask musician[s] to begin to play 'We plough the fields, and scatter'.) Why do we sing it? When do we sing it?

(Produce plough, which can be wheeled in up the aisle if it's a larger one!) What's today? Anyone ever heard of Plough Sunday? Why might we have such a Sunday? We have harvest, when we thank God for our food, but what happens to it before harvest-time? Go through likely dinner today—where has it all come from and how did it begin?

Preparation and sowing just as important as the harvest, so in country a plough was brought to church. It was and is the founda-tion of the farmer's work and represented the first job of the year. Plough Sunday was when God's blessing was asked on the work of the farmers for the year.

Remember the Bible reading? What happened to the farmer? Why? Left God out of reckoning. Farmers and the rest of us must remember our dependence upon God and show our gratitude to him.

(Perhaps look at ways in which your church can express this gratitude, eg, caring for others, giving to relief organisations, etc, and develop this theme a little.)

Plough Sunday may be a country thing, but in towns and cities we are just as dependent on God's goodness—and just as bound to thank him for it all.

Ian J Hutchings
Partington, Manchester

41 Missionary Sunday: The Drag-net

TEXT

Mt 13:47–50.

AIM

To teach that the gospel reaches many people, but that not all will be saved.

PREPARATION

Assemble props for the dramatic presentation: *a net*, ideally a proper fisherman's net, but a good length of lightweight garden netting with a suitable mesh size will be fine. Produce plenty of life-size *fish, made from cardboard*, drawn and coloured to look realistic. For extra authenticity, you may wish to copy from reference books of pictures of fish actually found in the Sea of Galilee. Write on the back of each, either 'good' or 'bad'. You will also need a *bucket* for the good fish.

PRESENTATION

This method of fishing is still practised in some parts of the world (eg, West Africa). The type of net used is a 'seine net'. One end is carried out from the shore by boat (demonstrate using your net). It is taken in a wide circle back to a point farther along the shore. Fish caught between the two ends are then trapped when the net is pulled in. As the last bit is drawn ashore, they can be seen struggling in it. (Get a helper to put your fish into the net.) Once ashore, the fish can be sorted out.

Now get members of the congregation to take out the fish one by one. If yours are copies of real ones, say what they are! Examine each one. Is it good or bad? The bad ones are thrown away, the good ones collected in the bucket.

Explain that God reaches out to many people with his love; all sorts and conditions are included. Jesus told his disciples that they would fish for men (Lk 5:10)—they were to win people for God, to become followers of Jesus. That is our job too, to seek to catch others for Christ. On the Day of Judgement those who truly follow Jesus will be separated from those who do not.

Steven Foster
Milton Keynes

42 Church Anniversary: Sure Foundations

TEXT

1 Cor 3:10–15; Eph 2:20–2 (Mt 7:24–7 is also relevant, better known, and could be used too).

AIM

To show the importance of building our lives (and that of our church) on Christ.

PREPARATION

Two tables are required, one firm and steady, the other less so (a folding card-table is ideal); a pack of playing-cards and a good supply of Lego, or better still, Duplo bricks. The tables need to be at the front where they can be seen.

PRESENTATION

Ask for volunteers (some may well volunteer before they know what for!), and invite forward two groups of three. If you can ensure that one group includes one or two argumentative members, perhaps brothers or sisters, so much the better. Set this group building a house of playing-cards on the less steady table, and the others building with the bricks on the other.

While this is going on, the Bible passages are read. (The action chorus 'The wise man built his house upon the rock' could be sung at this point by those not involved in the building work.)

Say something about why this is a special day for your church, then check on the progress with the two buildings. Looking at what has been done, comment that building successfully depends on three things:

1 Good foundations (compare the tables)

2 Good materials (compare the cards with the bricks)
3 Good teamwork (compare the two teams).

(Building work can now stop!)

Today we celebrate an important anniversary in the life of our church; and since the church means people, this means it's important for you and me. So there are some important questions we must face:

1 Are our lives built on the sure foundation of Christ as Lord?
2 Are we doing our bit for him, and being what he wants us to be?
3 Are we working together here as a team under him?

Ian J Hutchings
Partington, Manchester

43 Education Sunday (February)

TEXT

Eph 4:21–4 (NEB).

AIM

To show what 'learning Christ' means.

PREPARATION

You will need: (a) a bottle of correcting fluid; (b) one of your own school reports (or that of someone well-known to your congregation); and (c) some items of school uniform. If the items might be too small to be seen by everyone, even if you walk up and down the aisles with them, then they should be drawn on acetate sheets for use with an OHP, or made of card and displayed on a teazlegraph board.

PRESENTATION

Begin by discussing school: Do you like it? What do you enjoy most? Why do we have to go to school? etc. Lead conversation round to establishing that (among other things) we learn the truth, and we learn the right ways to do things. At school we learn about Jesus, but as we grow we should also 'learn Christ', as our reading reminded us when Paul spoke of 'how you learned Christ' (v 21). We can say we learn Christ just as we say we learn the truth or we learn the right way, because Jesus said, 'I am the way and the truth' (Jn 14:6).

Now the truth as it is in Jesus is that in life there is a right way to live and a wrong way. In our reading, Paul says that when one follows Jesus, one starts on the right way and one leaves behind one's old way of life. This new 'right way' is in three stages:

1   We must 'lay aside that old human nature' (v 22). (Show bottle

of correcting fluid.) Talk about what it is used for (blotting out mistakes). Jesus has blotted out our sins by dying on the cross. We can start with a clean page if we believe that Jesus died for us. 'We were baptised into his death' (Rom 6:3 NEB).

2 We must 'be made new in mind and spirit' (v 23). (Show report.) Quote anything on the lines of 'disappointing'; 'could do better'; 'shows little interest'; 'poor attitude', etc. As followers of Jesus, we have a new attitude to life; we live for Jesus and not for ourselves. We 'cease to live for sin and begin to live for righteousness' (1 Pet 2:24 NEB). If we live for Christ, we shall one day hear him give us the one report that really counts: 'Well done, my good and trusty servant' (Mt 25:21 NEB).

3 We have to 'put on the new nature of God's creating, which shows itself in the just and devout life called for by the truth' (v 24). (Show uniform.) Comment on how school uniform gives identity. We belong to such and such school. So, too, we belong to Christ and we are all part of him, just as together all the pupils make up one school. We are to put Jesus on like a uniform, so that others can see that we belong to him. People will judge a school by the way its pupils behave. As followers of Jesus, we carry his good name with us wherever we go. This is what is meant by being a witness. 'The life I now live is not my life, but the life which Christ lives in me' (Gal 2:20 NEB).

Conclude by emphasising that, as with all learning, the earlier you start learning Christ, the better. Ask: 'Have you begun to learn Jesus?'

David McIntosh
Ellesmere Port

PART TWO
The Christian Life

44 Family Worship

TEXT

'And the man Elkanah and *all his house* went up to offer to *the Lord* the
yearly sacrifice, and to pay his vow' (1 Sam 1:21 RSV).

AIM

To encourage regular family worship. The talk is suitable for
Mothering Sunday or for a service of Infant Baptism or both.

PREPARATION

If you are not a reasonably competent artist yourself, you will need
to delegate the artistic work required in this talk to someone who is.

Prepare the main OHP acetate sheet with the text above written
out at the top, but with three different colours to highlight 'all his
house', 'the Lord' and 'yearly'. Under this text and in the centre
write: 'They worshipped...'

Below that, on the left, have a small flap of acetate taped to the
left of the main sheet. On that write: '...the Lord' in the same colour
as highlighted in the main text above. Below it depict an empty
cross, perhaps with bright rays coming from it. Also include a tomb
with the stone rolled to one side.

Below this have another small flap similarly fixed with a selection
of common objects of modern worship, such as money, car, television, horseshoe. Have a further flap with a large cross (X) on it that
can cover these false objects of worship.

On the right-hand side of the main acetate and level with '...the
Lord', etc, have a flap attached to the right-hand side of the main
acetate with the words at the top '...as a family' in the same colour
as 'all his house' in the main text. Below this depict a family
consisting of father, mother and one child seated on a pew. Also
have another flap with the same child depicted alone on a pew. Have
a further flap with two crosses (X) on it, which when flapped over,
go on either side of the lonely child.

In the bottom right-hand corner of the main acetate opposite the objects of worship show a family worship book. Then attach a flap with the words '…in an ordered way' in the same colour as 'yearly' in the main text. On this flap also have a church notice-board, a calendar and a clock, each giving the details of your family services.

Most people use the OHP front projection on to an opaque screen. However, in church buildings it is often possible to project from the back, using a daylight screen made of translucent material (see Appendix). This has the particular advantage that the OHP, wires and even operator can be inconspicuous during the talk. The screen can be designed to be rolled up and down and suspended on a beam across the ceiling (if available). It can be let down during a hymn before the talk and the OHP put in place, guided by some chalk marks made on the stand prior to the service. It can all be removed during a hymn after the talk. The speaker should provide the operator with outline notes of the talk, so that it is obvious when to change acetates or move flaps.

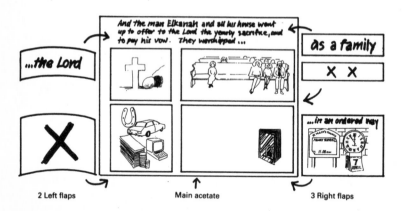

2 Left flaps   Main acetate   3 Right flaps

PRESENTATION

Explain that obviously our situation today is vastly different from the days of Samuel, 3,000 years ago. However, the Bible provides timeless principles to apply to our own day and age. Our text (switch on OHP to show it) relates to *three* things we are doing now (as the talk proceeds, flop over the appropriate flaps). Concerning Elkanah and his family:

1 *They worshipped the Lord*
Explain how we all worship something. In some parts of the world

> The heathen in his blindness
> Bows down to wood and stone
> (Bishop R. Heber,
> 'From Greenland's Icy Mountains').

In the West we may be more enlightened, but still have our gods.
Mention those on your acetate, like money, etc, pointing out the
futility of such worship and flop the cross (X) over them. Proceed
to explain that only the Lord is worthy of our worship (see Rev
4:11), and make reference to the crucifixion and Resurrection.
Stress that worship is no optional extra in our lives, but part of
the very reason for which we have been created. It will be our
continuous activity in heaven, so we should be getting into
practice now! For the Christian, it should be the spontaneous
response to the love and goodness of God.

> Praise, my soul, the King of heaven,
>   To his feet thy tribute bring;
> Ransomed, healed, restored, forgiven,
>   Who like me his praise should sing?
>   Alleluia! Alleluia!
> Praise the everlasting King!

2 *They worshipped as a family*
'...the man Elkanah and *all his house.*' Show how man and his
family are constantly linked in the Bible, such as Noah and his
family being saved in the ark, Jesus going to the Temple with his
parents and the promise of the Spirit, in Peter's Pentecost sermon, being given to parents and their children. Mention can be
made that in the Anglican and Roman Catholic marriage services couples are told that they are responsible for bringing up
their children in the Christian way; and in the baptism service
for infants it is assumed that parents will give their children the
help and encouragement they need by their prayers, teaching
and example. Statistics kept in Norfolk and in the South of

England before the Second World War showed conclusively that far more children continued in the Christian way when brought to church with their families than when sent on their own. (Flop two crosses over to show on either side of child.)

3   *They worshipped in an ordered way*
Elkanah and family went to make the *yearly* sacrifice. They went to a definite place, the temple at Shiloh, and at regular intervals. In New Testament days worship was weekly at the synagogue on the Sabbath, and it was Jesus' custom to go. The early church clearly had such a pattern, though probably in houses, as there were no church buildings in those days. Using the OHP visuals, outline your own worship to help families worship together regularly.

It is surely no coincidence that Samuel, the first of Elkanah and Hannah's children, grew up to become a great man of God, and when he died, the whole nation came to his funeral and mourned for him. May we all have the ambition for our children to become great men and women of God, by giving them the lead to worship the Lord as a family in an ordered way.

Michael Botting
Editor

45 The Family of God and the New Birth

TEXT

Jn 3:1–16; Acts 17:26; 1 Tim 5:8.

AIM

To teach about the family of God and how we become members of it by new birth. The talk is especially suitable for use at a baptism.

PREPARATION

Have a globe of the world, a dolls' house and an OHP. Prepare two acetates, both with complete circles which can be flopped over from either side of the OHP, so that they overlap each other a little. Mark on one of the circles 'THE WORLD' and 'SATAN THE PRINCE'. On the other circle mark 'THE KINGDOM OF GOD' and 'JESUS THE KING'. On a third acetate, which can be laid on the OHP from the start, draw a picture of a person who could be of either sex, so that it appears in the space where the two circles overlap.

PRESENTATION

The talk could be introduced with the story of the boy who was asked to write an essay on birth. He enquired from his mother about his own birth and was told he arrived by special postal delivery. Further enquiry revealed that his mother arrived in the world by stork. His grandmother was originally discovered under a gooseberry bush. The boy began his essay by declaring that there had not been a natural birth in his family for three generations! Ask the congregation of how many different families are they members? Attempt to discover the following three:

1 *The family of the world*
   Produce the globe and quote Acts 17:26 (he = God). We are all

one family because we all have been specially and wonderfully made by God. However, God loves us so much and knows we need special care, that he has also arranged for us to be members of another and smaller family.

2   *The family of the home*

Produce dolls' house and quote 1 Tim 5:8. God expects parents to make good homes for their children to grow up in. That will surely be true for you, or you would be unlikely to be here. Never forget to thank God that you have a good and loving home, because there are so many who have not these days. However, there is another family to which many here may belong, but possibly not all.

3   *The family of God the Father*

This family cannot be illustrated in the same way as the previous two, because it is only known by faith. We can show it to some extent on the OHP. When Jesus was talking with Nicodemus, as we heard in the Bible reading, he was really talking about two worlds—one we know very well.

(a)   *The world we live in that we can see all around us*

It has as its ruler Satan the prince. (Switch on OHP with that acetate showing, so that the circle includes the figure of a person. Speak about the mess the world is in.) Everyone is born into this world with a sinful bias, including little babies, as their parents will soon discover! We all share to some extent the awful state of the world.

(b)   *The world of the family of God the Father*

Jesus told Nicodemus about this world and said he had to be born into it. Nicodemus, and many people since, have found this a problem.

How are we born into God's family?

Because God made it possible. Tell the story of the snake in the desert and link it with the death of Jesus on the cross (Jn 3:14–16), so making forgiveness of our sins possible. We had no say about being born into our human family, but God does not force us to join his special family. We have an open invitation to join. If we decide to do so, we have to do two things: repent and believe. Enlarge on both and link with the responses in the baptism service. When we have done that, we gradually come to realise that God the Holy Spirit has come to work in our lives and we are members of God's special family. We have been born again.

Flop over the other OHP circle, and point out that we now find we are living in two worlds at once. Both Satan and Jesus will be wanting our allegiance. Refer to the baptismal statement that we should not be ashamed to fight under Christ's banner, but continue his faithful soldiers and servants to our lives' end. Conclude by questioning the congregation as to whether or not they are in all three families.

Michael Botting
Editor

46 The Gospel in a Nutshell (a crossword talk on Jn 3:16 GNB)

See page 31 for use of this talk.

See page 31 for use of this talk.

ACROSS

1 America is the new one (5)
3 (and 26) Change sex by decapitation (2)
4 Odd glove turned inside out (3,5)
9 An article? Definitely (3)
10 Ha! V-tube is broken (3,4)
11 More than four for the ancient Egyptians (4)
12 True Scottish dance, I hear (4)
14 ....'s 16 down: and nothing can be done (4)
17 Boy with no brothers (4,3)
18 Archaic of you (3)
19 Like (2)
21 These seven years were good (6)
23 To be certain of the things we cannot see (5)
25 A sweet age (7)
26 See 3 across (2)
27 Jesus tells us to leave it behind (4)
29 Gifts not wise men (5)
30 Graveyard tree (3)
31 Kingdom (5)

DOWN

1 Exclamation between points possess relative (3,3)
2 Directed (3)
4 All people (8)
5 Critical amount, but limitless? (2,4)
6 Creeps unnoticed (6)
8 Unfading wreath (7,4)
11 Month (3)
13 Threatening alternative (4)
15 16's end (2)
16 See 14 across (4)
20 Donated (4)
22 To dine in confusion is viable (3,3)
24 'Who would have thought the old man to have had so much blood _____' (2,3)
25 Killed (4)
26 Of him (3)
27 Bashful (3)
28 Before(3)

David McIntosh
Ellesmere Port.

1 WORLD 2 L D 3 HE
5 S H 6 S V
7 GODLOVED 8 E 9 THE
M H T E R
10 BUTHAVE 11 MANY
C S 12 R 13 EAL
14 THAT 15 T 16 T 17 ONLYSON E
18 THY 19 AS
20 G A 21 PLENTY 22 N
23 FAITH L O 24 I
V 25 SIXTEEN
26 HE 27 S 28 ELF D H
I 29 THREE I I
S 30 YEW 31 REALM

The Gospel in a Nutshell (John 3:16 GNB)

47 Invitation to Faith

2 Kings 5:1–19.

AIM

To show that we need to do things God's way, not our own, when we seek to be spiritually healed.

PREPARATION

You will need:

1 Four cups or mugs, one of them dirty
2 Two bowls, one filled with clean, cold water, and the other with warm, soapy water
3 Tea-towel.

Make one of the cups too dirty to be cleaned with cold water alone.

PRESENTATION

Story of the dirty cup (or oily hands)

Make up a story that tells how you were preparing a drink for your friends when you found one of the cups dirty (show dirty cup). Someone suggested that you wash it in cold water) try washing it in bowl of cold water—unsuccessfully). Then someone suggested that you try warm, soapy water. (After hesitation, and saying that it will not make any difference, wash it in warm water, which successfully cleans it.) A variation on this is a story about oil on hands not removed by cold water, but removable after oil-remover is rubbed into hands, then washed off.

The point is that the cup or oily hands could not be cleaned without the proper means.

The story of Naaman

Tell the story, explaining how Syria and Israel were in conflict and pointing out the social implications of leprosy. After Naaman's visit to the King of Israel, with all its pomp and show, note the contrast with the humble house of Elisha. The reluctant Naaman is persuaded to think again about Elisha's command, which called for selflessness, not showiness. Naaman is healed and returns to Syria grateful and committed to worship the living God, even though it will be difficult.

The ABC of this story

What are the actions of Naaman that led to his healing?

<u>A</u>DMIT   (i) Disease   (ii) Need of help
<u>B</u>ELIEVE   (i) Young girl   (ii) Prophet Elisha
<u>C</u>OMMIT   (i) Humility   (ii) Obedience

We have a picture of healing here that can be applied today to spiritual healing, because it speaks about our relationship with God.

Conclusion

Here we have a story of personal pride that must give way to God's grace. Not a matter of 'I'll do it my way', as Frank Sinatra sang, but listening to God's servants and spokesmen and doing it God's way.

Our ABC by way of application of the story to ourselves is as follows:

<u>A</u>DMIT our sin and need.
<u>B</u>ELIEVE the word of the Lord's people and leaders.
<u>C</u>OMMIT ourselves to the Lord in humility and obedience.

Ray Adams
Redditch

48 Supporters: A Baptism Talk

TEXT

Jn 21:15–22.

AIM

To show the roles to be played by parents, godparents, and the whole church in a baptism.

PREPARATION

Enlist the help of some fans of your local soccer team (or other sport) from your congregation, and arrange for one to bring a team strip and a ball, two or three to bring track suits of the appropriate colour, and up to half a dozen to bring all the supporters gear they can find: hats, scarves, rattles, hooters, etc. Have them slip out into the vestry or other room in the hymn before the talk to change, and wait for their cue.

PRESENTATION

Begin by talking about the local team's successes, taking care not to start a riot if rival teams are also represented!

Introduce the player, who comes in with a ball and bounces or dribbles it, etc. When the game is on, only the players are on the field, only they can play the game—it's up to them alone. So it is when a baby is baptised—only he can come to faith in Christ for himself, as he grows up, no one else can do it for him.

Introduce the trainers, who come in with track suits and who get the player to do some exercises. Behind the scenes there is a group of people who have special responsibility for the players: the trainers, physios, managers and other club staff. They are not on the field; they don't play the game; but they have a vital role if the players are to do well. This is just like the parents and godparents of a baby:

they show by example what it means to follow Jesus; they pray, they worship, they read their Bibles, etc, and support the child as he grows up.

Introduce the supporters, who make the predictable racket! Ask what it would be like for the players to go out into an empty stadium for a big match. The presence of a large crowd supporting and cheering their side on is a great asset to them, and the roar of the crowd urges them on. So it is with the whole church when a baby is baptised: we all have a role to play in praying, encouraging and 'cheering on' the baby and its parents and godparents.

Jesus told Peter he was to feed and tend his lambs and sheep; when new lambs are added to the fold, the whole flock carries this responsibility.

Ian J Hutchings
Partington, Manchester

49 Confirmation

TEXT

Eph 5:22–33 (NEB)

AIM

To show how being confirmed means entering into a lifelong relationship with Jesus.

PREPARATION

Draw the four pictures below on card for teazlegraph board, or preferably, on acetate sheets for OHP.

PRESENTATION

Begin by explaining why, when the subject is confirmation, the reading was all about husbands and wives—surely more suitable for a wedding—and remind congregation of Paul's words in verse 32: 'It is a great truth that is hidden here. I for my part refer it to Christ and to the church.' Point out that becoming a Christian is like being married: both should be acts of great responsibility; both demand total commitment. Explain how a Christian enters into a spiritual union with Jesus, just as a man and a woman enter into a physical union. Then go on to demonstrate how the stages in commitment are similar.

1 *Courtship*
   Discuss how a boy and a girl have to get to know one another; it may take a long time. So, too, a disciple has to get to know Jesus; talk about how this can be done.
2 *Engagement*
   The time comes when the boy and the girl are both sure that they love each other and want to be together for the rest of their lives;

each is willing to give up everything, if need be, for the other if only each has the other's love in return. They mark their decision to give themselves totally to the other by becoming engaged. Explain about knowing for sure that Jesus loves us—a love so great that he died on the cross to prove it—and wanting to love Jesus for ever in return; asking Jesus into our lives as Friend and Saviour.

3 *Marriage*

Talk about marriage service as couple's *public* declaration of their love and commitment; family and friends share in the joy of the celebration; a new 'Mr and Mrs' are welcomed into the community. So, too, a disciple of Jesus is called to declare publicly that he or she has given allegiance to Jesus; explain how this is done in confirmation—the laying on of hands is a symbol of how the work of the Holy Spirit has led the person to new life in Christ.

4 *Being faithful*

Emphasise that all said so far is only the prelude to actually living the rest of one's life within this special relationship. Explain, with reference to the fourth picture what 'for better, for worse; for richer, for poorer, etc' means in marriage. Point out similarity in Christian life: no guarantee of comfort and ease—rather the reverse—but God promises the strength to 'endure to the end' (Mt 24:13 RSV). 'This is the victory that has overcome the world, even our faith.'

David McIntosh
Ellesmere Port

50 Parties: Holy Communion

TEXT
Lk 22:7–20.

AIM

To teach the whole family about the meaning of the Lord's Supper,
though not necessarily in the context of a Communion service.

PREPARATION

For the lesson in this service, show the soundstrip 'The Secret
House' from the *Luke Street* series produced by the Scripture Union
Sound and Vision Unit (see Appendix for details). Have a small
table laid near where the talk is to be given, with bread on a paten, a
chalice and a bottle of wine.

PRESENTATION

Ask who likes parties. Did Jesus? How do we know? Why do we like
them? Aim to draw out that they are *fun*, and there may have been a
special element of that at the party we heard about in the soundstrip
because of the secrecy. Then it is a time to enjoy the company of our
friends, and Jesus said he particularly wanted to have this party with his
special friends, the apostles. Parties are also a time to enjoy special *food*,
and at Jesus' special party there was roast lamb, bread and wine.

Ask why we have parties? Aim to draw out that we usually have
them to celebrate special events, like birthdays, anniversaries or
Christmas. Mention that these are all to remember something
important. Hence point out that Jesus' party was to remember
something very special, even though it had not actually happened
yet. Draw out what that was. Finally, explain how we remember
Christ's death for us through broken bread and shared wine.

Michael Botting
Editor

164

51 The Church: The People of God

TEXT

1 Cor 12:12–18.

AIM

To explain simply that the Bible uses different pictures/analogies of the church to explain a particular aspect of the church.

PREPARATION

Use an OHP and show either (a) three pictures and words in sequence on one screen or (b) three pictures and words separately on the screen.

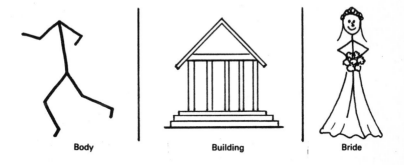

Body   Building   Bride

PRESENTATION

The church is understood in the Bible as God's people, chosen and called by Jesus to come and follow him. A people called out from the world, called together in the world, and sent out into the world. Only in a secondary sense is the church a building. Before the

Emperor Constantine embraced Christianity in the fourth century, Christians were not encouraged to build churches for themselves.

As we see from the writings of the New Testament, the church is to embrace young and old, black and white, rich and poor, intelligent and mentally handicapped, fit and sick, city, town and country. The church is for all ages, all nations, all cultures, for all times! Here are three pictures of the church given in the New Testament (there are others!).

The church is like a body

1 Cor 12:27. Key word: 'service'.

'We are the body of Christ.'

Human bodies have different limbs, organs and parts that all together make up the working body. Each part of the body has a different function but works within the framework of the human body for the body's growth, well-being and achievement. In the same manner the church is the body of Christ and under his headship should seek to serve him in a positive, constructive and fulfilling way.

The church is like a building

Eph 2:19–22. Key word: 'united'.

'One holy, catholic and apostolic church'.

The building in which the Lord dwells is composed of different stones of varying shapes, colours, sizes and functions. Expand on this in terms of people and their service in the church, seeking to provide local and universal application. The different denominations are all part of the one church, like columns in the building.

The church is like a bride

Rev 21:2. Key word: 'love'.

'God is love. Whoever lives in love lives in God' (1 Jn 4:16).

The church consists of people—all sorts, all ages, all backgrounds—and our common denominator is our relationship with Jesus our Lord. The picture of the church as a bride reminds us that our relationship with Jesus should be based on personal love. He loves us and we should love him in return. Within this love comes the commitment of faithfulness, purity and submission. The Song of Solomon in the Old Testament was an ancient love poem that was applied by Israel and later the church to a love relationship between the Lord and his people. So it should be that we love him because he first loved us, and so we are called to love one another and to love our neighbour as ourselves.

Conclusion

We are the people of God: the church. As a building, we must stand *united*; as a body, we must work together in *service*; and as a bride, we must live in a relationship of *love*.

Ray Adams
Redditch

52 The Christian Character: The Trinity

The idea for this talk is based on *More Assembly Services*, by R. H. Lloyd (The Religious Education Press, Ltd, 1975), p 45.

TEXT

1 Pet 1:15; 2:20b–1; Rom 8:14–15 (NEB).

AIM

To show how God as Father, Son and Holy Spirit together help produce the balanced Christian character.

PREPARATION

Obtain a real all-wooden cartwheel or wagon wheel, or draw one on as large a piece of card as possible. (The first place I used this talk was by coincidence a church dedicated to St Catherine; I did not have a real cartwheel, but there was one in every stained-glass window!) Also prepare cards with (1) 'Ever Loving Master', (2) 'Our Almighty King', (3) 'Active Spiritual Help' written on; the initial letters be larger or a different colour to stand out thus:

EVER	OUR	ACTIVE
LOVING	ALMIGHTY	SPIRITUAL
MASTER	KING	HELP

PRESENTATION

Show the wheel and discuss its composition. It is made of three different kinds of wood. They all have just three letters in their names. What are they? Having got the three answers, oak, ash, and elm, proceed to discuss the three parts, HUB, SPOKES, and RIM, in turn.

1   The HUB is at the centre of the wheel and must take a tremendous strain, so it is made of elm wood, which has a curved grain and will not split. Jesus must be at the centre of our lives for he is our Ever Loving Master (attach appropriate card). Peter reminds us (1 Pet 2:20b, 21): 'Your fortitude is a fine thing in the sight of God. To that you were called, because Christ suffered on your behalf, and thereby left you an example.' The Christian life is not easy—it cost Jesus his life to do God's will, but his example shows us how to stand up to all life's stresses and strains. 'I can do all things in him who strengthens me' (Phil 4:13 RSV).

2   The SPOKES on the other hand must not bend: they must be straight and rigid; so they are made from oak, which is one of the toughest and strongest woods. This speaks of God the Father who is perfect in power, in love and purity, for he is Our Almighty King (attach card). Again Peter tells us (1 Pet 1:15): 'The one who called you is holy; like him, be holy in all your behaviour, because scripture says, "You shall be holy, for I am holy." ' A Christian must try to be straight and honest in everything, because God's standards are perfect: he has made us to love him and glorify him in our lives. 'Stand firm and immovable...since you know that in the Lord your labour cannot be lost' (1 Cor 15:58 NEB).

3   The RIM has to cope with all the bumps and potholes of the road, so it must be yielding and a good shock-absorber, so it is made of ash wood, which is flexible. The Holy Spirit, Jesus has promised, will come and live inside all Christians and be their Helper and Strengthener. He will give us, as we go along life's road, Active Spiritual Help (attach card). Paul tells us: 'For all who are moved by the Spirit of God are sons of God. The Spirit you have received is not a spirit of slavery leading you back into a life of fear, but a Spirit that makes us sons' (Rom 8:14–15). So we need never be afraid: whatever happens, we can face it bravely; and whatever the circumstances, we can adapt ourselves and respond in the right way. 'I have become all things to all men' (1 Cor 9:22 RSV).

Conclusion

A person who is completely rigid and hard-hearted will be insensitive and unfeeling; one who is too soft may be ineffective in fighting for the right; one who is too tough will be unsympathetic. To be a well-balanced and complete character, we need a combination of virtues, just as the cartwheel needs a combination of different woods; in a similar way we need the help of God, Father, Son and Holy Spirit to be complete Christians.

David McIntosh
Ellesmere Port

53 Spiritual Warfare: A Motor-cycle and It's Master

TEXT

Mt 7:21.

AIM

To teach the need for regular servicing.

PREPARATION

Often we think too small when considering visual aids. For this, you will require a clean fully roadworthy motorcycle with its owner-rider and the full co-operation of other church leaders!

PRESENTATION

Begin by stating slowly and deliberately: 'Not every motor-cycle which says, "Owner, owner," will be able to give eternal service to its rider, but only those who have passed their MOTs!' (At this point the motor-cycle is literally ridden into the church and down the aisle to a suitable place at the front in good view, care being taken to anticipate any oil drips. The rider removes helmet and stands by to answer questions from the preacher.)

After making appropriate comments, proceed to draw out from the congregation—and the rider—what things can cause a motor-cycle to fail its MOT. As each item is named, add comments which will enable those with eyes to see and ears to hear to twig the spiritual lessons of the modern parable—write them up, perhaps, on an OHP.

Brakes	Running into danger, ahead of God, etc
Tyres	Skidding, sliding off the road, etc.
Steering	Especially in times of hazard and difficulty

Lights	Light, guidance to see where we are going
Mirrors	Watchfulness, for dangers coming up from behind us
Structural wear/rust **Mechanical wear/rust**	Need for cleansing and renewal
Clean oil/fuel	Need for refuelling, etc

When we humans come to Jesus, he rebuilds us. We start life as wrecks spiritually. But after becoming Christians, reconstructed sons and daughters of God, we need:

1 Regular cleansing
2 Regular servicing
3 Regular renewing
4 Regular refuelling.

We need to come to Jesus *regularly*—into the pits, as they say in racing—for:

(a) Cleansing from the impurities and corrosion of sin in the blood of Jesus
(b) Renewing of spiritual power and worn parts by the Holy Spirit of Jesus.

Not everyone who says, 'Lord, Lord,' enters the kingdom of heaven, but only those who come regularly to him for servicing and who go wherever he wants them to go.

Stewart Symons
Ardrossan and Irvine

54 Spiritual Warfare: The Armour of God

TEXT

Eph 6:10–18 (GNB).

AIM

To expound the significance of the various parts of the armour of God.

PREPARATION

Draw on card a Roman soldier, *at least* life-size, if not bigger, ensuring that the six pieces of armour as illustrated are clearly defined—helmet, breastplate, shoes, belt, shield and sword. If a drawing is used, prepare, in addition, labels for the six items of armour, which can be stuck on the drawing with Blu-Tack, or similar. Alternatively, better still, make or borrow a Roman soldier's costume as used in Nativity plays, for example. (A 7-piece set of Roman armour in moulded play-safe plastic is available from the Crusaders' Book Centre, 2 Romeland Hill, St Albans, Herts.) Arrange for a boy to wear it during your talk. The boy should be ready to indicate or hold up each item as required.

PRESENTATION

Begin by asking questions about soldiers in Roman days, then emphasise that the Christian is not fighting against human foes, but against evil and wickedness. The soldier needed just enough protection to enable him to avoid being hurt, without being weighed down and unable to get out of trouble quickly. So, too, the Christian armour is just what is needed to 'stand your ground when things are at their worst, to complete every task and still to stand' (v 13 NEB).

1 The belt of truth (v 14): the belt holds all together and gives

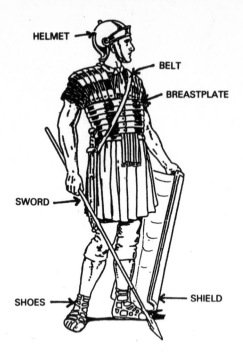

freedom of movement. Jesus is the truth and his service is perfect freedom: 'the truth will set you free' (Jn 8:32 GNB).

2   The breastplate of righteousness (v 14): guards the heart. The heart is a symbol of love, and 'we love because God first loved us' (1 Jn 4:19 GNB). A Christian is someone who is right with God; living in a secure relationship with a loving Father.

3   The shoes of the gospel: 'to give you firm footing' (v 15 NEB). Those who, like Mary (Lk 2:51), hide God's word in their hearts will be able to stand firm when all is chaotic in the heat of battle. Note:

> The words used carry the hint that warfare is not the complete description of the Christian's occupation—he is also a messenger with good news. There is also a beautiful paradox that, even in the midst of great struggle, the Christian has inner peace; Jn 16:33 (Francis Foulkes, *Tyndale New Testament Commentary on Ephesians*, p 175).

4 The shield of faith (v 16): to resist the temptation to give in. The fiery darts may be insults and accusations, impure thoughts and selfishness, doubt, fear and disappointment; so many things, but trust and obedience (which is faith) will render all attacks harmless.

5 The helmet of salvation (v 17): protects the head. Thus 'I know whom I have trusted, and I am sure that he is able to keep safe until that Day what he has entrusted to me' (2 Tim 1:12 GNB). We have the assurance of sins forgiven through the blood of Christ; and the hope of eternal life in Christ. Once we belong to Christ, we know also that 'nothing in all creation will ever be able to separate us from the love of God which is through Christ Jesus our Lord' (Rom 8:39 GNB).

6 The sword of the spirit (v 17): God's word is our only weapon of attack or defence in our Christian armoury. We have only to consider Jesus' use of scripture when he was being tempted to know that we too may similarly defend ourselves with conviction and power. If time permits, tell the story of David Wilkerson and his 'fight' with the bully, Chuck, in *The Cross and the Switchblade* (Marshalls: Basingstoke, 1963).

David Wilkerson, aged twelve, arrived at a new school, where he was informed that the school bully always beat up every new boy, and was particularly hard on 'preachers' kids'. David managed to avoid Chuck for a while, but eventually they met on a deserted street. David had prayed for God to give him a 'holy boldness' when faced with Chuck, and so when Chuck began circling him, preparing to fight and insulting him in every way he could think of, David kept repeating to himself the verse ' "Not by might, nor by power, but by my Spirit," says the Lord' (Zech 4:6 RSV). Chuck was completely baffled by this behaviour, and after throwing one very feeble punch, ran off. Next day, David began to hear how he had beaten the biggest bully in town. Chuck had been telling everyone that David was the toughest guy he'd ever fought.

David McIntosh
Ellesmere Port

55 Prayer

Lk 11:1–12.

AIM

To show how and why we can approach God in prayer, using the first sentence of the Lord's Prayer.

PREPARATION

Cardboard figures and lettering to be assembled on a visual-aid board. This talk could also be done with an OHP and acetates.

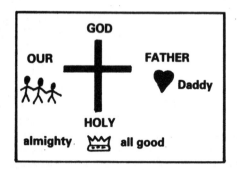

PRESENTATION

Introduce the subject of prayer, perhaps by talking about childrens attempts at prayer. (Add visuals as you talk about them to build up complete display.)

Prayer is about talking to | **GOD**

176

Verse 1–4. What is God called? Hallowed means| **HOLY**
Add a line to join GOD to HOLY.

What does Holy mean? | **all good** | Perfect.

and **almighty** The most important and powerful person in the world.

Talk about very important and powerful people.

(Add to represent power.)

What else is God called? **FATHER**

Talk to the children about relationships with parents. Things they chat about, share, etc.... (If family breakdown is high, talk about their ideas of good parents.)

If we have a good father, we may call him **Daddy**

Verse 5–8. Retell the story. Stress the importance of *asking* God for things.
Verse 9–10. Good parents only give us things that are for our *good*, not things that will harm us. Give examples.

To call God, Father and Daddy reminds us of his love.

In the Lord's Prayer, what sort of Father is God? **OUR**

To whom did Jesus give this Prayer? Disciples.
To all, God is Creator. To Christians, God is Father.
Who calls a person Father? Child.

Refer to and explain Jn 1:12. How do we become children of God?
When we receive Jesus.

(Add line to form a cross.)

We call HOLY GOD, OUR FATHER because of Jesus. This is why we usually end our prayers with the words 'through Jesus Christ, our Lord'.

Judith Rose
Gillingham, Kent

56 Take and Give

TEXT

2 Cor 9:15.

AIM

To show that giving should take place in two directions: we must receive from God but also give to him. The talk can be adapted for a special gift day, a baptism, harvest or Christmas.

PREPARATION

Find or make four boxes that fit into each other with reasonable ease. Cover the largest with gold paper and mark on it on different sides the word 'LIFE' and symbols to represent forgiveness (the word 'sin' with a cross over it) and the Holy Spirit (tongues of fire). The second box should be covered in silver paper and have symbols on it representing money, such as a £ sign and 7-sided coin with 50 in it. The third box could have pink day-glo paper on it with symbols representing different talents or abilities, such as music, sport, cooking, carpentry, etc. The smallest box should also be covered in bright paper and have a clock face on it. At the start of the talk all the boxes should be inside one another, so that only the largest is visible.

Also have two pieces of card, preferably red day-glo, 3″ or 8cm in width, and in length one 2′9″ or 84 cm and the other 1′6″ or 46 cm. With black lettering 2.5″ or 7 cm high and 1.5″ or 4 cm wide, put the word 'GENEROUSLY' on the longer strip vertically and the letters 'LOVI GLY' on the other strip horizontally. The two strips should then be joined with the shorter behind the longer with a suitable fastener, so that initially only the latter is visible, but when the smaller is turned into view, the word LOVINGLY appears, because the 'N' does service for both words, and the whole shape becomes a cross.

PRESENTATION

Ask who likes birthdays. Whose is the greatest? Why do we like such occasions? Encourage the word 'present' or 'gift' to be mentioned and so introduce the text. What was God's priceless gift? Why is Jesus so important? Refer to Jn 3:16 and talk about the gift of eternal LIFE, which we receive when we receive him as Saviour. Reveal your parcel and enlarge on the particular gifts of forgiveness and the Holy Spirit made possible through Jesus, showing the sides of the largest parcel. Ask the congregation if they have received God's priceless gift of Jesus and explain how. Parts of the baptism service can be quoted to help make these points.

However, when we receive gifts, we should normally be so grateful that we want to respond by giving in return, as a kind of 'thank you'. But what gifts do we have to offer God? Draw out from the congregation the following three ways, helped by the illustrations on the boxes, and comment appropriately:

1 Possessions, especially money. If parts of 2 Cor 8–9 have been read during the service, suitable parts could be quoted.
2 Abilities.
3 Time.

How should we give? Draw out from 2 Cor 9:6–7 the words 'GENEROUSLY' and 'LOVINGLY', and show the cross with those words on it. Finally, quote 2 Cor 8:9 and 9:15.

Michael Botting
Editor

57 Coins

TEXT

Mk 12:13–17.

AIM

To show how all that we are and have belongs to God. Suitable for a church anniversary or gift Sunday.

PREPARATION

Unlike most family-service talks, the visual aids for this talk require very little preparation. Find a large coin that might provide a focus of interest (I used a Maria Theresa silver dollar, but an example of the 'denarius' mentioned in the text would be ideal). It may also be helpful to prepare cards showing, in large letters, the full versions of inscriptions found on coins (eg, *Dei Gratia*, *Fidei Defensor*).

PRESENTATION

If there is to be a collection during the service, arrange for it to come *after* the talk. Read (or have read) the text above. Describe the coin mentioned and the way it was used to pay taxes. Show your own coin and explain its background, inscriptions, etc. Note in particular:

1   The coin bears a picture of a ruler
2   The coin is inscribed with the ruler's name.

Now ask the congregation what coins they have with them. This will probably produce some interesting specimens, as well as everyday coinage! Examine the coins. What is on them? (Your prepared cards may be helpful here.) Present British coins have both a picture and the name of the Queen. They are produced by her government, which also provides a police force, roads, schools, etc. That is why it is right to use our money to pay taxes, even if we don't like the government. (Think how unpopular the Roman government was!) Our coins bear the picture and name of our ruler.

Ask: 'Has anyone ever thought why we are called "Christians"?' Ask everyone to look at the person sitting next to him or her. If that person is called a Christian, he/she bears the name of Christ. For many people, the only picture they have of Christ is provided by Christians they know. Look more closely at your neighbour. A Christian: (a) should be a picture of Jesus; (b) carry the name of Jesus.

Think of the coins. Every coin shows the picture and name of a ruler. It belongs to the ruler and should be given to the ruler in the service of his/her government. Think of yourself. All Christians show the picture and name of Jesus. They belong to Jesus and should give themselves to Jesus to serve God.

Now give examples of how we can give ourselves to Jesus by the use of our money, talents, time, etc. This is what God wants, and it brings happiness and fulfilment to us.

Steven Foster
Milton Keynes

58   Gifts in the Church

TEXT

1 Cor 12:12–31; Is 6:8.

AIM

To encourage members of the congregation to discover and use their gifts.

PREPARATION

In stiff cardboard make a large jigsaw of eight pieces on which is the outline of your church. Attach Velcro to the back of each piece, so that they can be displayed on a teazlegraph board. In each of the eight pieces there needs to be a 'window' held in place by Sellotape, which can later be removed to reveal a word underneath.

'Windows' which can be removed to reveal words.

PRESENTATION

Choose eight children. Give each a piece to make the jigsaw. As they do this, explain that each child has one piece, but that they need to work together to achieve something. Compare this to the life of the church.

Make up a story of an imaginary family visiting your church for the first time. Show how the various gifts of the congregation can work together to enhance each member's visit. (An example of how this may be done is given below, but will need adapting to each church.)

Open window to reveal:

1	Whom will members of the family meet when they walk through the door? Talk about ministry of welcome.	WELCOME
2	What might the children be interested in? creche, Sunday school, etc.	LEADERSHIP
3	What might catch their eyes as members of the family sit down? Flowers, banner, posters.	ARTISTIC GIFTS
4	What will they hear as the service starts? Choir, music group, organist.	MUSIC
5	What else might the congregation contribute to the service? Led prayers, prayerful atmosphere.	PRAYER
6	After the service, how will they meet people? Coffee (NB: other gifts like gardening, cleaning and the difference they make).	PRACTICAL GIFTS
7	What might be given to them before they leave? Notice sheets, welcome leaflets, magazine.	HELPING
8	What might happen later that week? Lay visiting, pastoring.	VISITING

Would the family be likely to come again? Why? Everyone has done their part, so the whole family has met with God and been made to feel welcome.

What happens if one part is missing? (Remove a few pieces of the jigsaw one at a time and show what a difference it makes, if, eg, no music, or no welcome, no artistic gifts, etc.)

End by encouraging all to discover their gifts and use them.

Judith Rose
Gillingham, Kent

59 Gifts: A Talk for Gift Day, Christmas (or even the speaker's birthday or wedding anniversary), etc

TEXT

1 Cor 12:4–11.

AIM

To encourage the recognition and use of the gifts God has given us.

PREPARATION

The help of the speaker's wife or husband will be needed, as each has a gift for the other. For her, a pair of slippers. For him, a shoe box with rubber gloves, J-cloth, dish-mop and washing-up liquid. Both look similar on the outside, and are gift-wrapped. A supermarket product with a 'free gift' attached to it is useful, if there are any suitable offers on at the time!

PRESENTATION

Always sad in new year to see the small ads in the local paper selling variety of things, and describing them as 'unwanted gifts'. Strange, because we look forward to receiving gifts (and to giving them, I hope). Let's look at some of the different kinds of gifts there are.

Produce supermarket product with free gift (if you have one), and ask what one has to do to get the gift, ie, buy the main item. Everyone who meets that condition gets the gift; those who don't buy don't get the gift either. God gives a gift like that: the Holy Spirit. He gives the Spirit to all who ask Jesus into their lives: no Jesus, then no Spirit.

Give present to wife (receive if you are the wife!), and watch delight as it is opened and she says, 'These are just what I wanted.' There are some gifts that we know we want/need, and these things we pray for, such as patience, understanding, the ability to listen well, etc, and when God gives them to us, we also say, 'They're just what we wanted.'

Receive present from wife, and open with surprise as you extract and hold up each item. Ask what they are for, and what 'washing up' is, and why *you* have been given these things! We may not know we need some things until later on—but later we are glad we have them. Some of the things God gives us may seem a bit odd at the time, but in his time he will show us how we are to use them for him.

All these kinds of gifts are on offer. Are they just 'unwanted gifts' that we try to get rid of, or do we treasure them, seek after them and use them in God's service?

Ian J Hutchings
Partington, Manchester

PART THREE

Biblical Characters &
Miscellaneous Talks

60 Joseph (1)

TEXT

Gen 37; Rom 5:3–5.

AIM

This and the next talk illustrate, from the life of one man, how Christian character can be built up in times of hardship and suffering.

PREPARATION

For this talk you will need to prepare two OHP acetates as follows (see diagrams).

1 An acetate, blank except for Joseph in the bottom right-hand corner.
2 A blank acetate, but with flaps to be attached to the top (B), bottom (C) and right-hand side (A).

You will also need OHP pens during the talks. (Take a torch if you choose to use this method for the Morse code.)

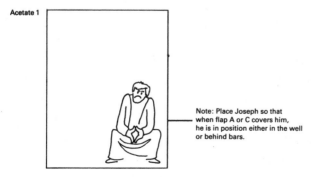

Acetate 1

Note: Place Joseph so that when flap A or C covers him, he is in position either in the well or behind bars.

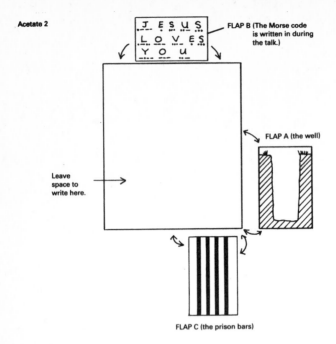

FLAP B (The Morse code is written in during the talk.)

FLAP A (the well)

Acetate 2

Leave space to write here.

FLAP C (the prison bars)

PRESENTATION

Introduce the family of Jacob. Put up acetate 1. Here is Joseph. Explain about his habit of having exalted dreams about himself. No wonder his brothers became jealous! He was also his father's favourite son. Describe the plot against him and how he came to be dumped at the bottom of the well (add acetate 2 with flap A). How do people think he felt?

Write up suggestions in the space on the left of acetate 2. Some of these feelings may be familiar to us. Often things happen to us that make us suffer—they can be hard to understand. Tap out this message (or flash it with a torch) .___ . ..._ ... .._.. ___ ..._ . ... _.__ ___ ... Does any one know what it means? Put it up on the OHP (flap B). As the congregation deciphers it, write the letters up over the Morse: 'JESUS LOVES YOU'. At first the message just seemed like a meaningless jumble of taps (or flashes), but in fact there was a message! And a wonderful one! Whatever happens to us as Christians, God is in control and is working out his plans for us. It may be hard to understand, but the love of Jesus surrounds us, even at these darkest times, and this is what he wants us to know. How much more should we know this, because we live on the other side of the cross to Joseph.

Steven Foster
Milton Keynes

61 Joseph (2)

TEXT

Gen 40; Rom 5:3–5.

AIM

See Joseph (1).

PREPARATION

Use OHP acetates as described in Talk 60. Add a third acetate, blank, but with flap D (the sleeping butler/baker) attached to the bottom, and flaps E (a,b,c) and F (a,b,c) attached to the top: E on the left, and F in the middle (see diagrams). NB: because of the many flaps, do practise and test this talk in advance!

PRESENTATION

Give a résumé of the story so far, using acetates 1 and 2 from previous talk. Eventually Joseph ended up in prison in Egypt (replace flap A with flap C on acetate 2). Again he felt hurt, betrayed, dejected, etc (suggestions written up on the acetate for Talk 60 last time). Before continuing the story, remove acetate 2 and replace with acetate 3, but with no flaps visible yet.

This is what happened when he was in prison: two others were in the prison, first the king's butler, then the baker, flap D. Tell the story of the dreams, the butler's first: the vine and branches (flap Ea), the blossoming and grapes (Eb) and pressing the grapes into the cup (Ec). Give Joseph's interpretation. Then the baker's dream (flaps Fa, b, c) and interpretation. Finish the story with the dreams being fulfilled, but Joseph still in prison (acetate 1 and 2 with flap C).

Despite his state and the future looking bleak, Joseph had learned a lot since his young, boastful days. He had learned that his dreams

Acetate 3

FLAP E
(a, b, c)

FLAP F
(a, b, c)

a — Vine in dream 'bubble' is bare.
b — Leaves and fruit are
shown—3 branches.
c — Juice drops into cup.

a — Man is holding baskets
(empty).
b — Bread is shown in
top basket.
c — Birds are shown
descending.

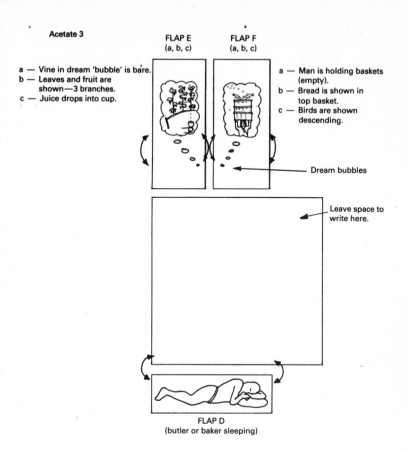

Dream bubbles

Leave space to
write here.

FLAP D
(butler or baker sleeping)

were not just to boost his ego but contained messages from God. He had learned to listen to God. (Write up 'Listen to God' in the space on the OHP acetate.) Although it had cost him his freedom, he had learned to remain faithful to God in adversity. (Write up 'Remain faithful'.)

The Lord can use our hard times to teach us and to build us into stronger Christians. In the end, Joseph was freed and reunited with his family. End by reading Rom 5:3–5.

Steven Foster
Milton Keynes

62 Moses and the Ten Plagues

Text

Ex 6:28 and 7:8–13.

AIM

To teach that God takes an interest in everything that goes on on Planet Earth, that sometimes he takes action and that his power is supreme.

PREPARATION

Ten cards will be required about 25″ x 5″ (64 cm x 13 cm) on which are written the words 'Blood', 'Frogs', 'Gnats', 'Flies', 'Anthrax', 'Boils', 'Hail', 'Locusts', 'Darkness' and 'Death'.

Also required for preachers without good memories—as the presentation must be fast—a cue card to fit their Bibles made out as follows:

1	Blood	Yuk!	Rod—hit river	River too high July/August
2	Frogs	Ribbet!	Rod—over ponds	River pollution/anthrax death
3	Gnats	Zzzzzz!	Rod—hit ground	High breeding due to river, etc
4	Flies	Swat		
5	Anthrax	Hold nose		Only animals in fields from frog contamination
6	Boils	Scratch	Dust in air	Skin anthrax from carrier flies Dec/Jan
7	Hail	Slap head (own!)	Hand to sky	Feb/barley & flax

8	Locusts	Click tongue rapidly	Hand to sky	March/wheat & spelt Locusts bred from upper Nile
9	Darkness	Hand over eyes	Hand to sky	Khamsin wind
10	Death (of first-born)	Eldest fall to ground		Uniquely supernatural

PRESENTATION

God takes a close interest in all that happens on planet earth. Usually, he lets us sort things out ourselves—as mums and dads let their children. Sometimes he takes action—as mums and dads do when their children fight.

One day God became very angry with a cruel king called a Pharaoh. Pharaoh was forcing people to work for nothing, and he was murdering all their baby boys, while he himself lived in great comfort and wealth. God said, 'Enough is enough—time to act.' (At this point ask for ten volunteers to hold the cards. Get them to come to the front, but do not give out any cards yet. They should stand in a row facing the congregation, with elbow room. Also tell the whole congregation that you want them to take part, too: (a) by making the appropriate sound or doing the appropriate action whenever the word on the card is mentioned; (b) by shouting a loud 'NO' whenever you say, 'Did Pharaoh let them go?')

The first action God took through Moses after the initial skirmish in our opening reading was to turn the water of the River Nile to blood (give first card to first volunteer and get everyone to make the appropriate sound). (If you wish, you can fill out the dramatic detail by indicating Moses' action and the 'natural' conditions which would tie in with the miraculous event—adults especially will note the knock-on effect, the devastation upon Egypt's economy and the timing leading up to the time set by God for the Passover as you proceed through the ten plagues.)

Proceed briskly through the full sequence of the ten plagues, with periodic recapping. For example, after the first three, which are all sound effects you can say, 'Now how far have we got? Ah, yes! First there was the river to blood, then the frogs, then the gnats...', and at the mention of each of these words everyone makes the noises again. 'And did Pharaoh let them go?' 'NO,' everyone shouts, etc. (You will now see the reason for the cue cards.)

This is a fun presentation, but the seriousness can be all the more tellingly brought home when you come to the tenth plague, when the divine hand is so much more in evidence, and when you describe God's secret instruction to his people for their safety from judgement with the blood of the lamb on the doorposts and strength for the journey with the lamb's meat roasted and eaten.

Pharaoh was a tough nut to crack! It took ten decisive acts on God's part, but God did it! And God rescued his people.

If you wish, you now sing 'My God is so big, so strong and so mighty'.

Stewart Symons
Ardrossan and Irvine

A Six-week Holiday Series on David the Shepherd King

The following six talks are designed to follow the showing of the six soundstrips with the above title, published by Scripture Union (see Appendix). They could be used as a holiday series beginning, say, on the last Sunday in July and continuing to the first Sunday in September, depending on the number of Sundays in August. The soundstrips themselves could be used in place of the Bible reading in the family service, since they are clearly based on biblical stories. A daylight screen can be used, as referred to in the Appendix. The filmstrip itself has to be put into the projector back to front as well as upside-down.

63   The Shepherd Boy

TEXT

Ps 23.

AIM

To show that in all the problems of life God can be trusted. The talk is particularly suitable to be used at a baptism.

PREPARATION

Set up an OHP for front projection on to a screen. Prepare two acetates in advance, having at the top one of the two headings printed below. On a third acetate draw a large cross in red, crucifixion-shaped, that covers most of the acetate. On a fourth acetate draw the outline of a conventional heart. Have an OHP pen available and a scribe who can write reasonably quickly and legibly.

PRESENTATION

Refer to the soundstrip 'The Shepherd Boy' and to David, who was to become one of the great men of God in the Old Testament. Like us, even when only a youth, he was to discover:

We live in an evil world (acetate 1)

Ask the congregation, especially the younger members, what evils David was aware of, and expect answers like bears and unkind brothers. Write these down briefly on the first acetate. Also add other evils that we are aware of today. Ask how David coped with his problems. Mention that when we were baptised, we were told to fight valiantly against the world's evils of sin, the world and the devil. However, we know so much more than David because we know who has been victorious over all evil. Ask who. And how. Place the large cross on the third acetate over the evils on the first acetate. Remove both.

We live in God's world (acetate 2)

Refer to David's parents, who obviously brought him up to understand that this evil world is not all. Though unseen, behind it is God, who can be trusted and should be worshipped. This is seen in the Psalms, many of which were written by David, especially the twenty-third. If Bibles are available, get people to suggest the good things we can learn about God from this psalm, and write them briefly on the second acetate.

Ask what the psalm shows about David's relationship with God, and draw out that he obviously trusted him in a personal way. Mention that in the baptism service we are asked to believe and trust in God the Father, who made the world, Jesus, who died for us, and the Holy Spirit, who gives us new life. Ask whether everyone really does, explaining that belief is more especially with the mind, but trust is with the heart. Place the outline heart on the fourth acetate over the second.

Michael Botting
Editor

64 The Heart of the Matter

TEXT

1 Sam 16:7.

AIM

To show that God knows us as we really are.

PREPARATION

The second soundstrip from *David the Shepherd King*, entitled 'Who Will Be King?' should be shown before the talk. If you feel you require further visual material, the following words/phrases could be put on a teazlegraph board or OHP when referred to in the talk: 'THE CONTEXT', 'THE CHOICE', 'THE CONTRAST', 'Sam was sad', 'Sam was scared', 'Sam was surprised', 'trust', 'obey'. Pictures of a face, home, money and car would also be useful.

PRESENTATION

We all long to be chosen. Get from, or suggest to, the congregation examples: school team, new job, marriage partner, etc. The great Old Testament leader and prophet Samuel, whom we heard about in the soundstrip, had that problem.

The Context

Tell the story of King Saul: tall, handsome, strong, an obvious leader, *but disobedient and rejected by God.*

Sam was sad

Explain how God told him to stop moping and *do* something, namely to anoint another king. Mention that most monarchs are anointed at their coronations, and refer to the British Queen's in 1953. Refer to the soundstrip.

Sam was scared

Explain how Samuel was afraid King Saul might kill him if he heard he was about to plan his replacement. So he was told to go to Bethlehem to offer a sacrifice, like a religious service, and invite all Jesse's sons.

The choice

In recapping the story, or drawing it out from younger members of the congregation, mention that, of course, Saul was also a fine-looking man like Eliab. But God does not judge by outward appearances. Refer to the fact that we all do the same, assessing people by their face, home, money, car. (The author must admit that he tended to be put off a potential curate, because of a ring in one ear! Similarly, his teenage daughter normally wore very ancient jeans on most occasions, including to church. She was also concerned about what her friends thought of her, which they would partly judge by her clothes. Besides, her father was a vicar, so it was even more important that her friends should think her normal! When challenged about her church attire by members of the congregation, she replied in words at the heart of today's talk: 'Man looks at the outward appearance, but [God]...looks at the heart.')

Sam was surprised

Continue the story and Samuel's surprise at finding no suitable son to be king. Hence recap the choice of David. Why was he chosen? Not because he was perfect, or no one would be chosen, but because God knew he was humble, a man who would *trust* and *obey*.

The contrast

God judges inwardly, man outwardly. Refer to 1 Cor 1:27f, and illustrate with such people as Gladys Aylward, the servant-girl, who became a missionary to China, and Cliff Richard, who continues to be in the forefront of pop-singers, when secular singers have disappeared from the public arena without trace. None of these people is perfect, but humble enough to admit his or her sins, accept God's forgiveness, and trust him in the big and little things in life.

Conclude by saying that this is what God is looking for in us. If we, like David, will humble ourselves before God and trust and obey, we too can be one of the chosen—where it really matters.

Michael Botting
Editor

65   David and Goliath

TEXT

1 Sam 17.

AIM

To help understand how we can cope with temptation. This talk is particularly suitable to be used at a baptism.

PREPARATION

The third soundstrip from *David the Shepherd King*, entitled 'Goliath,' should be shown before the talk. Words could be put on a teazle-graph board or OHP, namely 'GOLIATH' (deliberately in upper-case), 'David', 'envy', 'anger', 'hate', 'belief' and 'trust'. A 'House of David Bible News' cassette is available on the David and Goliath contest, part of which could be usefully played during this talk (available from Bible News Ltd—see Appendix for details—or order through your local Christian bookshop).

PRESENTATION

GOLIATH (place name in the top left-hand corner of board or screen) was over 9′ tall. Indicate that height with reference to something clearly visible to the congregation. His armour and spear together would weigh as much as a grown man. Imagine him putting it on, swaggering and boasting, hero-worshipped by small Philistine boys daring to get his autograph! A Rambo character, more brawn than brain. There is evidence of his having brothers of similar height from skeletons of giants found in the area of Gath. In 2 Sam 21:20ff there is reference to these giants having deformed hands and feet, and this deformity is known to include extreme short-sight, which may mean that Goliath simply did not see David's stone coming at him. Such an idea simply had not entered his mind before! However, neither David nor Saul's army would have known that, when he came out each day to challenge them.

What is our Goliath? Fear? That was certainly Saul's problem. More likely our major Goliath is temptation to sin. Like Saul and David's brothers, we can nurse *envy*, which can lead to *anger* and *hate* (put on board or screen under GOLIATH). But no doubt there are many other temptations as well. Baptism is all about this and our need to fight valiantly against sin, the world, and the devil.

David (place in the top right-hand corner of board or screen) lived in Bethlehem, fifteen miles from the battle zone. In those days there was none of the media coverage that we take for granted today. Had there been, it might have sounded something like this. (Play part of the cassette referred to under PREPARATION.) David's father used his youngest son as go-between to keep him up-to-date about how the war was going, and also to provide extra rations for his soldier sons, perhaps with some extra for the commanding officer to encourage promotion for them. Continue to recap the story from the soundstrip by questioning the younger members of the congregation. Why was David so successful? Because his trust was not in worldly armour, but in the strength that God gave, that he had proved when fighting bears and lions. Baptism is all about *belief* and *trust* (place these words under *David* on board or screen), when we publicly commit our lives into God's hands, believing and trusting that he will defend us from our Goliath of temptation to sin, the world, and the devil.

David's meeting with Goliath was no chance event: it led directly to David becoming king. God had permitted the contest. Years later, Jesus was led by the Spirit into the wilderness to be tempted by the devil. God permitted the contest. James, in his New Testament letter writes that we should rejoice when we are tempted. God is allowing it, and as we apply our belief and trust in him, like David and Jesus, we shall have the victory and God will especially bless us.

Note

The *Guinness Book of Records* states that the tallest man in the world was Robert Wadlow, an American, who when he died at the age of 22 in 1940 was 8'11.1" tall, and his armspan was 9'7.5". He weighed 31st 5lbs. *Guinness* also says that according to biblical measurements Goliath was 9'6.5", but the Jewish historian Josephus (AD 37/38) and some manuscripts of the Septuagint attribute to Goliath the more credible height of 6'10".

Michael Botting
Editor

66 The Singer

Rom 8:28: 'And *we know* that in all things God works *for the good* of those who love him. . . .'

AIM

To teach that however adverse our circumstances may seem, God's purposes will be fulfilled in our lives if we trust him.'

PREPARATION

Write out the text for all to see, with the five words highlighted as above.

PRESENTATION

Refer to David the singer in the soundstrip 'The Singer' and remind the congregation that David wrote many of the psalms, including one of the most famous, namely the Shepherd Psalm, 23. Tell the true story of a Swiss shepherd who had a young shepherd boy to help him with the sheep on the hills. The shepherd was a Christian who taught his lad to remember that the Lord was his Shepherd, and, to emphasise the point, spelt out the first line of psalm on the boy's thumb and fingers, stressing the 'my' on the fourth finger. Comment on the text in four parts:

1 *'we know'*
   Like Paul, who wrote our text, and David who wrote the psalm, the shepherd had come to know the Shepherd of whom the psalm speaks. One day there was a very heavy fall of snow on the Swiss hills. The boy had gone out to look for the sheep and got lost. After a big search he was found dead, but he was holding his

206

fourth finger tightly with his other hand. He also had come to know the Shepherd, and so can we.

2 *'that in all things God works for the good'*

We do not always understand why God works in a particular way, for instance, why that boy should die. However, in the case of David, we know God had willed he should become king, so despite Saul's jealous fury and evil schemes, David was always spared.

3 *'for the good'*

Obviously David was not without problems, due to man's sin, especially Saul's. Most, if not all, God's people have troubles. Perhaps tell briefly the story of Joseph the dreamer and refer to Gen 50:20, stressing that despite Joseph's suffering caused by his brothers, God intended it 'for the good'.

4 *'of those who love him'*

This promise is only for God's followers, like David and Paul and all here who know Jesus as Saviour and Lord. God offers no hope for those who go against his will.

Consequences

So what does this verse hold out to those of us who follow Jesus into this new week? Whatever troubles the future may bring, we know it will be for our good. We trust in God's love. So we are not going to 'touch wood': we don't believe in superstition, nor are we going to worry. (See Mt 6:34.)

We began with a story about Ps 23 and we will end with one. Hence relate the story of the actor who recited that psalm at the end of an important banquet and was given a tremendous ovation. A bishop present was then asked to recite the same psalm, but got no applause. Asked why the difference, the actor replied, 'I only knew the psalm; the bishop knew the Shepherd.'

Michael Botting
Editor

67 Friends: David and Jonathan

After using the fifth soundstrip of David ('Friends') I pointed out that despite Saul's hatred for David, David never retaliated, but only offered Saul respect and love. It therefore seemed appropriate to adapt a talk by Peter Bannister entitled 'From hate to love' in *For All the Family* (Kingsway 1984), of which I was editor. For those who have not got the book, I very briefly summarise.

Using four (or nine) children to hold the letters H-A-T-E-G-V-I-L-O, you move from HATE to LOVE, changing only one letter at a time, and commenting on six relevant texts as you proceed. The words and texts are as follows:

HATE (Jn 3:20), GATE (Mt 7:13), GAVE (Gal 2:20), GIVE (Mt 10:8 AV), LIVE (Phil 1:21), LOVE (1 Jn 4:19).

Michael Botting
Editor

68   The Outlaw (or the cave of Adullam)

Text

1 Sam 22:1–2.

AIM

To draw a parallel between those who joined the army of David in the cave of Adullam and those who join the army of Jesus, great David's greater Son. This talk is particularly suitable at a baptism, at which it was originally given.

PREPARATION

The talk does not lend itself very well for visual aids, though the showing of the sixth part of the soundstrip ('Outlaw') and the baptism itself are obviously visual enough. The main and sub-headings could be put on an OHP.

PRESENTATION

Refer to Saul's murderous hatred of David, due to jealousy. David escapes to the mountains around Bethlehem, where he was brought up. These mountains are famous for their caves. He hides in the cave of Adullam and is joined by 400 men, over whom he becomes captain. We have here a very appropriate parallel with baptism, when we sign on for the army of Jesus Christ and promise to continue his faithful soldiers and servants to our lives' end.

Three things were true of David's captaincy that are also true of Jesus':

1   *They were in need (v 2)*
    Each need has Christian application:
    (a)   'In distress'—Enlarge on matters that distress your con-gregation, from bullying at school to family problems and the rat

race. See Mt 11:28.

(b) 'In debt'—We are all in debt to God because of our sins, but Jesus has paid the debt on the cross: 'There was no other good enough to pay the price of sin...'

(c) 'Discontented'—Refer to the things that people crave for in this life, which ultimately bring no lasting satisfaction. Then refer to Jn 10:10b.

2 *They were few (v 2)*

Only 400 compared with the thousands in Saul's army. Refer to Mt 7:13–14. After 3 years' ministry, Jesus was deserted, and only left 11 men at his Ascension. Paul told the Corinthians that not many wise or important people follow Jesus. Jesus never boasted that many would follow him, because there is a cost. That is why at baptism we are challenged not to be ashamed to confess the faith of Christ crucified.

3 *David made a mighty army of them*

The small band grew, David was honourably victorious over his enemies and eventually became king of Israel and Judah. Jesus calls us to make him our captain in our fight against sin, the world and the devil. His may have been a small army at the beginning, but people have been joining it for the past 2,000 years—the greatest army in world history. In baptism we are going to enlist one more member into its ranks.

As we watch this baptism, may it remind us of our own Christian commitment to the army of Jesus Christ. Men and women who joined the allied armies during the second World War knew it would be for twenty-four hours a day, seven days a week. They were promised blood, sweat and tears for an uncertain victory. Can we offer anything less to the Captain of our salvation, the King of kings, in a fight where victory is assured?

Michael Botting
Editor

69 Grace and Mephibosheth

TEXT

2 Sam 9.

AIM

To teach the meaning of grace, and to use the story of David and
Mephibosheth to illustrate it.

PREPARATION

Read up the whole story of Mephibosheth, so that you can retell it
vividly to children without notes. You will need to cover the following passages at least in preparation: 2 Sam 4:4, 9:1–13, 16:1–4,
19:24–30, 21:1–7. You will obviously not use every detail, but knowledge of the whole is necessary so that what you do say does not stray
from the truth.

To pinpoint the message also prepare some transparencies as
indicated below.

PRESENTATION

---

1 GRACE

The name of a girl
What we say before we eat
A prayer of blessing used in church.

LOVE AND HELP WE DON'T DESERVE

---

2 AN EXAMPLE OF GRACE

How King David treated Mephibosheth
1 David gave him sonship
2 David gave him safety
Mephibosheth could expect neither.

**SONSHIP and SAFETY were given to Mephibosheth
BECAUSE OF David's LOVE for Jonathan**

---

3 THE SUPREME EXAMPLE OF GRACE

How God treats Christian believers
1 Sonship with Almighty God
2 Safety from eternal death are given to us.

BECAUSE OF God's LOVE for Jesus

GRACE = LOVE and HELP we DON'T DESERVE

Stewart Symons
Ardrossan and Irvine

70 Jesus, the Way

TEXT

Jn 1:35–42 and 14:6.

AIM

To show how we can find the way to Jesus and that he is the way through life and to God.

PREPARATION

You will require: a teazlegraph board, ideally two-sided; some cardboard figures backed with Velcro; lettering on cardboard arrows; powder paint and a brush for ladder lettering.

PRESENTATION

Talk about how we find our way to places.

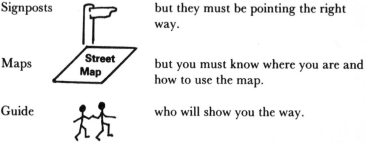

Signposts — but they must be pointing the right way.

Maps — but you must know where you are and how to use the map.

Guide — who will show you the way.

John the Baptist

Was like a signpost saying, 'Follow him'. This is the role of the preacher, who can point the way to Jesus.

John also had something else with which to point people to Jesus. He called Jesus 'The Lamb of God'. The disciples knew what that meant because it was in their Bible (Old Testament). The Bible points to Jesus.

Bible ⟩

John also pointed his friends to follow Jesus. Christian friends can point us to Jesus.

Friends ⟩

So preachers, the Bible and Christian friends can all help us find.... (Turn the board around or uncover other side. Then, using ladder lettering, put in the letters to form 'JESUS')

The way through life

Life for us may be good and happy (give examples) or difficult, eg.... How do we know what to do when we have big decisions to make or when life is empty, or when there seem to be no standards in life? Jesus said, 'I am the way.' He gives us guidelines about home, friends, money, work, illness, etc. (Put up symbols to represent these things.)

The way to God

Jesus is also the way to God: 14:6 (explain).

Judith Rose
Gillingham

71 Jesus, the Healer

TEXT

Mt 5:21–5.

AIM

To show how Jesus brings healing to the whole person: body mind and spirit.

PREPARATION

Draw on large card the three pictures below (or use OHP): (a) trees walking; (b) pigs; (c) branch and fruit of the sycamore fig tree. Prepare cards (or separate OHP sheets for overlay) with SALIVA, LEGION and TINY written on them.

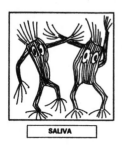  

PRESENTATION

Show each picture in turn and ask for comment; add the words to the appropriate picture to provide a clue to the incident each represents. Ask questions until the three stories have been identified. Then tell in your own words the stories of (1) the blind man (Mk 8:22–6), (2) Legion, the Gerasene demoniac (Lk 8:26–39), and (3) Zac-

215

chaeus (Lk 19:1–10), emphasising in (1) the physical healing, (2) the mental healing, and (3) the spiritual healing.

Conclude by stressing the importance of spiritual healing for all: many are fully fit, physically and mentally—and if not, Jesus still has the power to heal—but everyone needs to be put right with God; like Zacchaeus, we need to respond to Jesus' love, admit our sins, believe that Jesus will accept us and give us eternal life.

David McIntosh
Ellesmere Port

72 Bartimaeus and Christ, the Healer

TEXT

Mk 10:46–52.

AIM

To demonstrate the implications of salvation through Christ by means of the story of the healing of Bartimaeus.

PREPARATION

Prepare words and illustrations to cover three vertical and three horizontal sections of a teazlegraph board, as shown below:

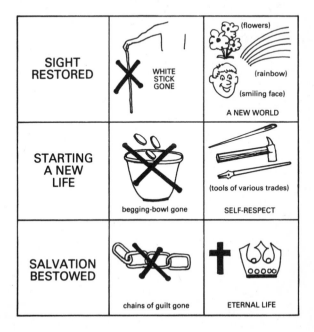

PRESENTATION

Retell the story of Bartimaeus, and emphasise the three different levels on which his life was changed as you build up the illustration on the board.

1   What did Bartimaeus want? To have his SIGHT RESTORED. Jesus gave him his sight because he knew that Bartimaeus believed that Jesus could do so. Jesus always responds when we ask in faith and trust him.

2   What difference did it make to Bartimaeus? He could throw away his white stick (meaning his old way of life was gone). He was no longer an outcast.

3   A whole NEW WORLD was now open to him; he could see flowers, rainbows, smiling faces! What a wonderful experience that must have been!

4   Bartimaeus would have immediately realised that he would now see his whole life change; indeed he was STARTING A NEW LIFE.

5   He could throw away his begging-bowl. No more days of sitting at the side of the road, calling out into the blackness for people to have pity on him and throw him some scraps of food.

6   He could now work for a living and regain his SELF-RESPECT.

7   Jesus not only gave him back his sight, but he gave him SALVATION as well; for we heard at the end of the story that Bartimaeus began to follow Jesus.

8   Bartimaeus knew that not only was he physically better but his sins were forgiven: the chains of guilt were gone.

9   Now he began a life of discipleship: he had taken hold of ETERNAL LIFE.

Conclusion

Our lives may never be as dramatic as Bartimaeus', but we can share in the discoveries Bartimaeus made when he encountered Jesus. Paul reminds us that 'when anyone is united to Christ, there is a new world' (2 Cor 5:17 NEB). Life as a disciple of Jesus is a fully satisfying life: 'I have come that men may have life, and may have it in all its fullness' (Jn 10:10 NEB). And finally, all who put their trust in Jesus will have eternal life and one day be with Jesus for ever in heaven: 'God loved the world so much that he gave his only Son, that everyone who has faith in him may not die but have eternal life (Jn 3:16 NEB).

David McIntosh
Ellesmere Port

73 The Healing of the Official's Son (a crossword talk on Jn 4:46–53 GNB)

Jesus went back to Cana in 1 down (7). An official was there whose son 12 down (4) ill, in 6 across (9). When he heard that Jesus had come from Judaea to Galilee, he went to him and asked him to go to Capernaum and heal his son, who had been 4 across (5) ill, and was about to die. Jesus said to him, 'None of you will 5 down (4) believe unless you see 9 across (7) or a 10 down (4).' 'Sir,' replied the official, 'come with me before my child 16 across (4).' Jesus said to him, 'Go, your son will 14 across (4).' The man 7 down (8) Jesus' words and went, without 4 down (7) to look back once. On his way home his servants came 11 across (7) to meet him with the news, 'Your boy 13 down (3) recovered.' He 15 across (5) what 8 across (4) it was when his son got better, and they gave the 3 down (6): 'It was at one o'clock yesterday afternoon when the 12 across (5) left him.' Then the father 2 down (10) that it was at that very hour when Jesus had told him: 'Your son will live.'

David McIntosh
Ellesmere Port

The Healing of the Official's Son
(Jn 4:46–53 GNB)

74 Jairus' Daughter and the Woman Who Touched Jesus (a crossword talk on Lk 8:41–56 NEB)

Then a man appeared—Jairus was his name, and he was president of the synagogue. Throwing himself down at Jesus' feet, he begged him to go to his house, because he had an only daughter, about twelve years old, who was 28 across (5). And while Jesus was on his way, he could hardly 9 down (7) for the huge 1 down (5) of 25 down (3) and women.

Among them was a woman who had suffered from 20 across (12) for twelve years; and nobody had been 16 down (4) to 26 across (3) her of her disease. She came up from 9 across (6) and touched the edge of the special 1 across (7) Jesus used to 10 across (4) as a rabbi, and at once that was the 29 across (3) of her illness. Jesus asked, 'Who was it that touched 25 across (2)?' All disclaimed it, and Peter and his companions said, '4 across (6), the crowds are 17 down (7) you in and pressing upon you!' But Jesus said, 'Someone did 11 across (5) me, for I had a 19 down (7) that 18 down (5) had gone out from me.' Then the woman, seeing that she was 12 across (8), came trembling, her face a very pale 2 down (3) with fear, and fell at his feet. Before all the people she explained why she had touched him and how she had been instantly 22 down (5) of her 15 down (7) illness. Jesus 3 down (6) at her and said, 'My daughter, your faith has cured you. Go in peace.'

While he was still speaking, a man came from the president's house with the message: 'It's no 30 across (4), your daughter has 24 down (4), the Master no longer 8 down (5) to trouble himself further.' But Jesus heard, and interposed. 'Do not be 14 down (6),' he said, 'only show faith and she will be well again.' On arrival at the house, he allowed the child's father and mother to go into the room, along with Peter, James and John, but he 5 down (4) all the 7 down (5) people out. And all were 27 across (7) and lamenting for her. He said, 'That's 6 down (6) crying; she is not dead: she is asleep.' But all they did was 13 across (5) at him, well knowing that she was dead. But Jesus took hold of her hand and called her: 'Get up, my child.' She came back to 21 across (4) and stood up 23 across (11), and he told them to give her something to eat. Her parents were astounded; but he 4 down (4) them promise not to tell anyone what had happened.

David McIntosh
Ellesmere Port

Jairus' Daughter and the Woman Who Touched Jesus (Lk 8:41–56 NEB)

75 Matthew Levi

TEXT

Mt 9:9–13.

AIM

To draw out some important lessons from the life of this most unlikely disciple of Jesus, using a very simple visual aid.

PREPARATION

Make four large cards having on them each of the letters L E V I.

PRESENTATION

Warn the congregation that the leader is going to be using four-letter words today! Ask four children to come out to the front and give each of them the letters to spell LEVI.

Mention that Matthew occurs, in all the lists of the apostles of Jesus, but in Mark and Luke's gospels he is referred to as LEVI. Only Matthew refers to himself as a tax-collector. Since they were regarded as Jewish traitors and were hated and despised, out of kindness Mark and Luke avoid mentioning it.

Matthew and Jesus both lived in Capernaum, which was an important trade route, so that customs-house officers, like Matthew, would have their hands full. It is more than likely that Jesus and Matthew knew each other quite well.

Ask if the congregation think Levi was a good man? On receiving the answer that he was not, get the children to move to spell: EVIL. Refer to the fact that tax-collectors in those days always took more than they should. Money ruled Levi's life, and Jesus taught: 'You cannot serve God and money' (Mt 6:24). But then Jesus also taught that we are all evil (Lk 11:13). It is because of this that we need the gospel, one of which Matthew Levi was to write.

But he was more than just evil. He was also: VILE. Get children to move to spell that word. As we have seen, he was not just dishonest, but also a traitor. It is all the more surprising, therefore, that Jesus called him, and that he should follow, though he cannot have enjoyed the loneliness and unpopularity of his job. But God often calls the worst. Refer to Saul of Tarsus and perhaps people you know.

Later Levi was to write about what Jesus had done for him as a Jew. Get the children to move to spell: VEIL. Enlarge on the significance of the rent veil in the Temple when Jesus died on the cross.

Lastly, get the children to move to spell LIVE. Matthew Levi was so thrilled to live for Jesus he threw a party. Refer to Mt 9:10–13.

Suggest that we might have been shocked to see the company that Jesus kept. Could we be trusting in our very respectability to earn our place in heaven? We may not be living vile lives, like Matthew, but God sees us all as evil, and so just as much in need of a Saviour as him. Like Matthew:

> We are writing a gospel, a chapter each day
> In all that we do and in all that we say.
> People read what we write, whether faithless or true.
> Pray, what is the gospel according to you?
>
> (Source, unknown)

Michael Botting
Editor

76 Zacchaeus (a crossword talk on Lk 19:1—9 GNB)

Jesus 14 down (7) 6 across (7) and was passing through. There was a 3 down (5) tax-collector there named 8 across (9), who was very 2 down (4). He had made his 23 across (7) fortune by having cheated the people for 19 across (4). He 12 across (6) to see who Jesus was, but he was a little man and could not see Jesus because of the crowd. So he ran ahead of the crowd and 3 across (7) a 20 across (8) tree to see Jesus, who was going to pass that way. When Jesus came to that place, he looked up into the 4 down (8) and catching Zacchaeus' 24 across (3), he said to him, 'Hurry down, Zacchaeus, because I must stay in your 10 down (5) today.' Zacchaeus 9 down (7) down the 25 across (4) and 1 down (8) him with great joy. This caused quite a 20 down (4), as many of the people were 19 down (5) at what Jesus had 26 across (4). 'We 18 down (6) to know why he has gone as a 22 across (5) into the 10 across (4) of a sinner.' Zacchaeus stood up and said to the Lord, 'Listen, Sir! I will give 7 across (4) my belongings to the poor, and if I have 17 across (7) anyone, I will pay him back four times as much.' But Jesus, who 13 across (11) everyone's thoughts, 5 down (8) Zacchaeus and in order to 16 down (7) him said, 'Salvation has come to this house 15 down (5), for this man, also, is a descendant of Abraham. The Son of Man 21 down (4) to seek and to save the 11 down (4).

David McIntosh
Ellesmere Port

		1 W		2 R		3 C	L	I	M	4 B	E	5 D
	6 J	E	R	I	C	H	O			R		E
		L		C		I			7 H	A	L	F
8 Z	A	C	C	H	A	E	U	9 S		N		E
		O				F		H		C		N
10 H	O	M	E		11 L		12 W	I	S	H	E	D
O		E			O			N		E		E
13 U	N	D	14 E	R	S	15 T	A	N	D	S		D
S			N		T	O		E			16 H	
E			T			17 D	I	D	18 D	L	E	D
	13 A	G	E	S		A			E		A	
	N		R		20 S	Y	21 C	O	M	O	R	E
	22 G	U	E	S	T		A		A		T	
	R		D		23 I	M	M	E	N	S	E	
24 E	Y	E		25 T	R	E	E		26 D	O	N	E

Zacchaeus (Lk 19:1–9 GNB)

77 The Wedding at Cana
(a crossword talk on Jn 2:1—11 GNB)

Two days later there was a <u>6 down</u> (7) in the town of <u>15 down</u> (4) in <u>27 across</u> (7). <u>28 across</u> (5)' mother was there, and Jesus <u>19 across</u> (3) his disciples had also been invited to the wedding—there were presumably family <u>26 across</u> (4). When the <u>11 down</u> (4) had given out, Mary <u>30 across</u> (4) rather <u>12 across</u> (3) at ease, and came in quite a <u>29 across</u> (5) to Jesus and said to him: 'They have no wine left.'

'You <u>16 down</u> (5) not to tell me what to do,' Jesus replied. 'My time has not yet come.' Jesus' <u>3 down</u> (6) then told the servants, 'Do whatever he tells you.' The Jews have rules about <u>1 down</u> (6) washing, and for this purpose six <u>18 across</u> (5) water jars were there, each one <u>23 across</u> (5) enough to hold about a <u>10 across</u> (7) <u>13 down</u> (6). Jesus said to the servants, '<u>24 across</u> (4) these jars with water.' They filled them <u>19 down</u> (3) to the brim, and then he told them, 'Now draw some water out and <u>4 across</u> (4) it to the <u>8 down</u> (3) in charge of the <u>2 down</u> (5).' They <u>5 down</u> (7) <u>7 down</u> (4) with the water, which had now turned into wine, and the man tasted <u>17 across</u> (2). He did not know where this wine had come from (but of <u>9 across</u> (6), the servants who had been <u>20 down</u> (7) the water knew). So, having drunk <u>18 down</u> (4,3) wine, he called the <u>7 across</u> (10), and said to him, 'Everyone else serves the best wine <u>24 down</u> (5), and after the guests have had plenty to drink, he serves the ordinary wine, but you have kept the best wine until now!'

Jesus performed this first <u>14 across</u> (7) in Cana in Galilee; there he revealed his <u>22 across</u> (5), and his disciples saw the <u>25 down</u> (5), and began to <u>21 down</u> (7) in him.

David McIntosh
Ellesmere Port

The Wedding at Cana (Jn 2:1–11 GNB)

78 What It Means To Forgive One Another

Philemon.

AIM

To explain from the letter of Paul to Philemon what it means to forgive one another and bring about reconciliation.

PREPARATION

You will require a teazlegraph board and the words 'Love', 'Forgiven/ess', 'Philemon', 'Onesimus' and 'Paul'. Make a poster, as shown below, and a large postcard with a drawing of a red heart on the back and the following words on the front:

From	Paul
To	Philemon
About	Onesimus.

You should also make a symbol of the cross for use on the teazlegraph board. Put up symbol, words and poster as the talk develops.

234

PRESENTATION

The cross

(Put up the symbol of the cross on the board.) Remind everyone that love is the foundation of Christianity (Jn 3:16). This love is from God to people and from people to people. It involves both the understanding and practice of: (a) being *forgiven* (put up word); (b) showing *forgiveness* (extend the word by adding 'ess'). Jesus taught us to forgive: Mt 6:12 and 18:21–35. Jesus showed us how to forgive: Lk 23:32–4.

The story of Philemon

(Put up poster.) Retell the story of Onesimus, the runaway slave. Slaves were wanted, dead or alive!

Three characters involved (put up names):

> Philemon —the rich Christian leader
> Onesimus —the runaway slave
> Paul —the Roman prisoner.

Paul sought to put matters right, so he sent a very short letter to Philemon—more like a picture postcard of early Christian life (show the card). What do we learn about early Christianity from this 'postcard'?

1 Christianity was establishing a new society, on the basis of love; instead of hate, there was to be salvation. This meant action not just words.
2 The lessons of forgiveness:
    (a) Someone had to forgive—Philemon.
    (b) Someone had to say sorry—Onesimus.
    (c) Someone had to make peace—Paul.
    Truly to understand and practice forgiveness, there are times when we must stand in each of these men's shoes.

Christianity is a life-changing religion, so by the power of God's spirit within us let us take the teaching and example of Jesus to heart and:

(a) Do the right thing—Philemon.
(b) Say the right thing—Onesimus.
(c) Encourage the right thing—Paul.

Ray Adams
Redditch

79 Onesimus: A Really Useful Disciple

TEXT

Philem 1–16.

AIM

To show what we must do to be really useful disciples.

PREPARATION

You will need a Thomas the Tank Engine toy, or picture of any of the best known railway engines from the Revd W Awdry's books, or use a tape of one of the stories. Also needed is a broken battery-powered clock (or similar).

PRESENTATION

Show Thomas the Tank Engine (or play tape). Discuss the ambition of all the engines to be called, by the Fat Controller, a 'really useful engine'. But things often went wrong for them.

Is there anything in your house that is really useful? Do they all work? (Ask for examples of something that ought to be really useful but isn't.)

Show clock. It's no use because it doesn't work. What can we do? Either (a) Throw it away; or (b) mend it, if possible. ONESIMUS was in a similar position. His name means USEFUL, and he should have been useful to Philemon, but he wasn't, and Philemon was very likely to punish Onesimus severely or abandon him because he had run away. But he was useful to Paul, so Paul wanted to 'mend' him, if you like: restore him to usefulness to his master. We don't know why Onesimus ran away—there is a suggestion later in Paul's letter that he might have stolen from his master—but meeting Paul changed his life and he became a Christian; Paul wants Onesimus to have a new start and therefore appeals to Philemon to accept Onesimus as a Christian brother.

Look at the clock again. Why doesn't it work?

1 No batteries, perhaps? We will be useless without the power of the Holy Spirit.
2 Worn out? We will be useless unless we are daily renewed through prayer and Bible study.
3 Damaged or neglected or misused? Unless we put Jesus first in our lives, we will end up damaged and spoiled. If we want to be really useful, we must allow Jesus to control every aspect of our lives.

Onesimus needed putting right (Paul helped to do that); he needed forgiving, and he needed to return home. The very fact that this personal letter became attached to the other letters Paul wrote and included in the New Testament is proof that Philemon *did* accept Onesimus back. Point out the parallel between this story and that of the prodigal son: that God our Father loves us all, however bad, is always ready to forgive, and will give us every opportunity to be really useful to him every day of our lives.

David McIntosh
Ellesmere Port

80 The Good Samaritan
(a crossword talk on Lk 10:30–7 GNB)

Jesus answered:

There was once a man who was going down from 9 across (9) to 6 down (7) when 14 down (7) attacked 3 down (3), stripped him, and beat him up, leaving him half dead. It so happened that a priest was going down that road; but when he saw the man, he turned away 15 down (6)—because he was afraid he might 4 down (6) himself by touching a dead body—and walked on by on the 18 down (5) side. In the same way a 8 down (6) also came along, and he 3 across (5) his eyes from the sight of the injured man, and walked on by on the other side. The man must by this time have wondered, 'Would no 26 across (3,4) to help him?' But a 7 down (9) who was travelling that way came upon him, and when he saw how much he was in 24 across (4) of help, his heart was filled with pity. This was remarkable because Jews used to look down upon and 20 down (5) at Samaritans. He went over to the man and began 21 across (8) his 2 down (6), pouring 26 down (2) oil and 16 across (4) from a 23 across (4) on them. He 27 across (4) up his shirt to 10 across (4) his cuts and bruises. When he had 10 down (8) the man, he 20 across (3) him on his 1 across (3) 12 across (6) and 19 down (5) to an 22 down (3), where he took care of him. The 13 across (4) 25 down (3) he took out two silver coins and gave them to the innkeeper. 'Take care of him,' he 5 down (4), and when I come back this way, I will pay you whatever else you spend on him.'

And Jesus concluded: 'In your opinion, which of these three acted like a 17 across (4) neighbour towards the man who was in danger of his 8 across (4)?'

The teacher of the law answered, 'The one who was 11 across (4) to him.'

Jesus replied, 'You go, then, and do the same.'

David McIntosh
Ellesmere Port

Completed crossword grid (clue numbers shown in brackets where printed):

```
■    ■    O(1) W(2) N    ■    ■    ■    H(3) I    D(4) E    S(5)
■    J(6) ■    O    ■    S(7) ■    ■    L(8) I    F    E    A
J(9) E    R    U    S    A    L    E    M    ■    F    ■    I
■    R    ■    N    ■    M    ■    V    ■   B(10) I    N    D
K(11)I    N    D    ■    A(12)N    I    M    A    L    ■    ■
■    C    ■    S    ■    R    ■    T    ■   N(13) E    X   T(14)
A(15)H    ■    ■   W(16) I    N    E    ■    D    ■    ■    H
G(17)O   O(18)D(19) ■    T    ■    ■    S(20)A    T    ■    I
H    ■   T(21) R    E    A    T   I(22) N    G    ■    ■    E
A    ■   H(23) O    R    N    ■   N(24) E    E   D(25)  ■    V
S    ■    E    V    E    ■   O(26) N    E    D    A    R    E
T(27)O    R    E    ■    ■    N    ■    R    ■    Y    ■    S
```

The Good Samaritan (Lk 10:30–7 GNB)

81   The Prodigal Son
(a crossword talk on Lk 15:11–24 GNB)

Jesus told this parable, which is a story with a spiritual 3 across (5).
There was once a man who had two sons. The younger one said to
him, 'Father, give me my 34 across (5) of the 21 down (8) now.' So
the man made the 23 down (3) decision: he divided his property 15
across (7) his two sons. After a few days the younger 22 down (7)
sold his part of the property and 18 down (4) home with the 37
across (5). He went to a country 32 down (3) away, where he wasted
his money in 24 across (8) living. He would have been 2 down (4) to
have put his money in the bank, but he 28 across (5) and 28 across
(5) until he had 8 across (4) at all. Then a 19 down (6) famine spread
over that country, and he was faced with the choice of poverty or 27
down (4), as all his friends 14 down (8) him. How he began to 6
down (3) the day he had left home! How ashamed he must have felt
when he was forced to 31 down (4) himself out to one of the citizens
of that country who 5 down (3) him to work minding pigs. He
wished he could fill himself with the 29 down (4) pods the pigs ate,
but no one gave him anything to eat. At last common 26 down (5)
prevailed and he said to himself, 'I 1 down (4) do something.' Then
the 13 down (4) struck him:

> All my father's 30 across (5) 16 down (7) have more than they
> can eat; 25 across (5) I to 38 across (4) here and 26 across (6)?
> I will get up and 36 down (2) to my father and say, 'Father, I
> have sinned against God and against you. I am 9 down (2) 4
> down (6) fit to be called your son; make 3 down (2,3) of your
> hired workers.'

So he made a 5 across (5) on the journey back to his father.
   Although it did 11 down (4) 20 across (10) to his father that he
would ever see his son again, he went out every day in the hope of
seeing him; and so one day, when the boy was still a long way from
home, his father saw him and his heart was filled with pity when he
12 across (7) how thin and weak he looked. He ran to him, threw his
arms round him and gave him a 17 down (4). 'Father,' the son said,

'I have sinned against God and against you. I am no longer fit to be called your son.' But the father called his servants.

> Hurry! Bring the best robe and put it on him. Put a 35 across (4) on his finger and 10 across (5) on his feet, then go and get the prize calf and kill it, and let us 33 across (9) with a feast. For this son of mine was dead, but now he is alive; he was lost, but now he has been found.

And happy to be 7 across (8), the feasting began.

David McIntosh
Ellesmere Port

The Prodigal Son (Lk 15:11–24 GNB)

PART FOUR
Parade Services

Introduction

Two shoe salesmen were sent by their employers to work in a new country, and on their arrival they discovered that the inhabitants just did not wear shoes. The first sent a message to his office: 'Am returning home. No market for shoes here.' The second also sent word home: 'Send extra supplies. People do not yet wear shoes. Wide-open market.'

One saw the task as a waste of time; the other saw the great opportunity it presented. It seems that these two views are also to be found when we look at parade services. To some they are a burden, and the use of the time is questioned; to others they are a great opportunity, for here are young people sitting right where we want them, ready for whatever we are going to say and do in church.

Uniformed youth organisations seem to be part of our way of life. Scouts and Guides, Boys' Brigade and Girls' Brigade, Compaigners, Church Lad's and Church Girls' Brigade, Cadets for the Army, Navy and Air Force... the list seems endless. Most of these groups have in common their custom of having a regular parade service, usually monthly, and it is to that monthly parade that I address myself. How do we see it? How do they see it?

If we see nothing but a burden, then we are selling the young people short. It is certainly true that there is no easy way with parade services—no short cut.

And the young people themselves... how do they see their parade service? In a recent (and admittedly small) survey among the organisations with which I am involved, three companies said they looked

247

forward to their parade service, six said they put up with it, and one admitted to avoiding it. If that pattern is general, the story is a sad one indeed.

Several other questions are raised by the survey. Should the parade take place in a Holy Communion service? Should it not have a special shape of its own, perhaps along the lines of Morning Prayer? Is it not a valuable occasion for a visual-aid talk? What are we to do, particularly as we are dealing with significant numbers of people without any great church connections, and whose Christian understanding is, therefore, limited? How do we fit them in? How do we make them feel welcome?

Interest

With band playing and colours on parade, numbers of young people march into our churches for 'their' service. Stimulating and maintaining interest in the service seems an obvious place to begin, but it demands careful thought. The first essential is to take time and trouble to understand the organisations, so that their particular needs and backgrounds are catered for.

For example, most will probably only be in church when there is a parade service, so any continuity from one week to the next is made difficult. Similarly, some will be members of Sunday-school groups and such like, but many will not. We can make few assumptions about what they know and what they are used to, particularly when the organisation concerned has no specifically Christian constitution.

Holding this interest, then, is more than slotting a lively talk into a service otherwise unaltered from what happens every other Sunday, when young people are elsewhere. We need to look at the relevance of everything we do, to choose music with great care, to ensure that what happens is capable of being understood and actually *enjoyed* by those on their monthly parade. There is, however, always the danger of taking this too far, of planning the service as if the organisation members were the only ones there—forgetting the rest of the church family, whose needs are just as valid. It is a wide interest for which we are looking.

Involvement

Another key word in looking at parade services is 'involvement', which means a two-way commitment.

First, there is the involvement of the organisation in the worship, and in the life of the church generally. It may be that one of the uniformed members will occasionally be asked to read a Bible passage; perhaps two might hand out books or take the collection. Yet although these are a good start, by themselves they would reflect a purely cosmetic solution to the problem of involvement. We have to do better than this if we really mean 'business' with these groups.

Many organisations will have members with musical ability: can they help with (or sometimes take over) the leading of the singing? Brass instruments from bands can often add something special to our hymns; others may play guitars, recorders, etc, all of which can be used to add new dimensions to our worship.

Drama in worship is another area where involvement can be developed. There is a wealth of good, simple but effective material available today, much from the Riding Lights Theatre Company, and its use to illustrate readings and talks can be very effective. What better than to ask members of an organisation who already meet, and who already know each other, to plan and perform a sketch from time to time? (See Appendix for ideas, and please take care to observe the copyright restrictions shown in each publication.)

Some organisations will lend themselves to the planning and leading of prayer times, too. If there is perhaps a link missionary, or if the church is sponsoring a special project, there can be scope for the young people to be involved with keeping information up-to-date and presenting it to the rest of the church. They could also lead imaginative prayer in both the organisation and the parade service.

Involvement goes beyond the monthly parade, too. Are there some practical tasks around the church and grounds for which the young people could be responsible? Please be realistic in what you suggest, and don't ask them just to do the rotten jobs! Depending on their Christian commitment, is there a share in pastoral care they could take on—visiting housebound folks, designing and delivering publicity, or helping with work with younger children? Leaders of uniformed organisations are frequently on the look-out for opportunities for community-service projects and ideas for group and individual activities, particularly for badge-work or for such things as the Duke of Edinburgh's Award. The list seems endless!

Involvement goes the other way, too. It is vital for the church to be involved with the life of the organisation. Maybe some (or all) of the leaders are church members who see their involvement as part of their ministry, and in the end this is a crucial factor. Leaders may have much to offer in many ways, and may be 'sympathetic' to the monthly parade, but if they are not church members, real involvement will not follow.

A large number of members of the church family can also contribute to the life of the organisation. Most organisations undertake a considerable variety of badge-work—if they can find the people to teach and test the work. Who could be involved to do some basic cookery, woodwork, needlecraft or sport? Who might help with the ever-present problem of transport from time to time?

The active interest of the minister in the organisation is a great help in maintaining the involvement of the church, too—not just in looking in for five minutes, and perhaps leading prayers, but as part of the whole life of the group. It is no bad thing if he can perhaps do some badge-work (and not just Bible knowledge, etc), join in supporting teams at sporting events, and even go to camp if possible, as his gifts and time permit. It hardly needs saying that young people and their leaders will respond far more enthusiastically if they know the minister is really interested in them as people rather than as once-a-month 'pew fodder'.

Equally important in the church's involvement with the youth organisation is the way in which the latter is seen by the lay people, particularly by the governing body of the church. Some of the older lay people may boycott the parade services because they can't cope with the noise and bustle of the youngsters. This is a perennial and difficult problem, which may sometimes be overcome by trying to arrange it so that old and young can meet on a one-to-one basis, rather than in a more intimidating group. Some of the questions asked earlier about how the parade is seen by the rest of the church could well be looked at in this sort of context, and the discussion could pave the way to better understanding.

Uniformed groups are often left to do their own thing, with little awareness and, therefore, little interest from the church leadership. If the young people are not seen as part of the church at that level, there is little hope of their feeling that they belong, and this will be reflected in the attitude they take to the parade service. Some imagination may be needed to overcome this problem, but one useful suggestion is to persuade the organisation to hold an informal open evening for church leaders, and then lean on them to attend! It's amazing how understanding and tolerance can be fostered over the table-tennis table or chatting at the coffee bar.

Incorporation

Interest and involvement must lead on to incorporation, from being taken seriously to being part of the church. The youth organisation must be incorporated into the whole body of the church, and both organisation and church must accept this as a natural thing. This will then be reflected in the worship which takes place at parade services, as the whole church values and is enriched by what the young people bring, and vice versa. This may be easier with an organisation which has a specifically Christian constitution, but it can be achieved with others, too.

The parade service has somehow to fit into the general pattern of the whole life of the church as well as into that of the organisation. Any such dove-tailing is intricate work that takes time and patience. Teaching will be needed to prepare each half of the equation for the other. But in the end, the body can be brought together, each part being itself and offering its own contribution to the whole, to the glory of God.

Ian J Hutchings
Partington, Manchester
Assistant Regimental Chaplain
The Church Lads' and Church Girls' Brigade
Chester Diocesan Regiment

82 Owls and Brownies

TEXT

Mt 7:24.

AIM

To get a basic and memorable message across to a district gathering of Brownies and Brownie leaders.

PREPARATION

Prepare transparencies for OHP as per diagrams below.

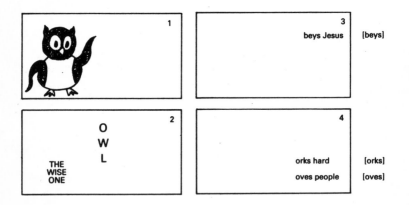

PRESENTATION

What, I wonder, does a normal Brownie think of first—when, for example, putting on her Brownie uniform? I don't know, but if I were a Brownie, I should imagine it must be OWLS: Brown or Tawny! (Show diagram of owl outline.)

When thinking about what to say on this special occasion, I looked up the word 'owl' in the Bible and also in the dictionary.

Dictionary: 'Night bird of prey; wise-looking solemn person.' Not much help there. Not very flattering either! The Bible wasn't much better! There were just about four references. Bible: 'Owls are not to be eaten' (2); 'Owls live in ruins' (2). One positive thought there: owls know the art of survival!

So we'll pick up that thought and fasten our attention on the folklore image of owls being wise! (Superimpose 'The wise one' and 'O W L'.) The wise one obeys Jesus. (Superimpose 'beys Jesus'.) Why? Because Jesus said that those who hear his words and obey them are like a wise man building his house on a rock. Only those with a faith in Jesus and who obey him will survive the troubles of this life and possess eternal life in heaven when this life is over.

It also follows that if one is wise and obeys Jesus, one will work hard and love people. (Superimpose 'orks hard' and 'oves people'.) I looked another word up in the Dictionary—'Brownie'. Dictionary: 'Benevolent sprite/elf/fairy; haunting houses; doing household work.' What a super definition! I guess our Brownies here would enjoy haunting houses, they probably do; but what about household work, I wonder? Are they wise to work hard and love people?

We have been fortunate to have had an excellent succession of wise owls—Brown and Tawny—over the years at this church; and I believe most Brownies have grown up to love people and work hard, some as housewives. May God long continue to bless our church and its Brownie pack, and long may its Brownies be wise owls!

Stewart Symons
Ardrossan and Irvine

83 The Greatness of Service
(Suitable for a Scout service, with appropriate adaptations for Guides)

TEXT

Mk 10:35–45.

AIM

To show from the teaching of Jesus that true greatness involves service.

PREPARATION

You will need to make a series of enlarged 'badges' copied from the Scout manual to represent badges such as, craftsman, camper, pioneer, explorer, life-saver; also a 'service flash', 'Patrol Leader flash' and 'Assistant Patrol Leader flash'.

PRESENTATION

Talk about what they think it takes to be a great person. Use examples of well-known people from history and the present day. How many of you would like to be known as Fred or Simon or Kevin the Great?

Who was the greatest man that ever lived? Popular pictures of Jesus sugget a weak, feeble person. But if Jesus had been a Scout, he would have had badges like these (hold up each enlarged badge in turn and explain why Jesus qualified) eg, craftsman (His craft was? Carpentry); camper (He often slept out in the open).... To get these badges you need to be tough and strong. Summarise the text in your own words.

Jesus compares the world's standards of greatness with his own, and challenges them to follow his example. If Jesus were a Scout, he would also have many service badges. Ask who has service badges and how many. (Hold up a service flash.) 'Great men,' said Jesus, 'roll up their sleeves and help others. They give their lives serving others.' NB: part of the Scout promise is 'To help other people'.

If you do well, as you grow up you will be given more responsibility, ie become more important, eg, Scout Leader, Patrol Leader (hold up Assistant Patrol Leader and Patrol Leader flashes). These responsibilities are not given for you to be bossy, order others about and do all the easy jobs, but so that you can serve others and do the difficult and dirty jobs for them. We are given responsibility or made important FOR SERVICE.

NB: part of the Scout promise is 'To do your duty to God'. One of the things that that means is to become more like Jesus, who was tough and strong and served others. To become like Jesus is to be on the way to being a really great person.

Judith Rose
Gillingham, Kent

84 Hats

TEXT

Eph 6:17; Deut 6:8; 1 Pet 5:4.

AIM

Using the idea of the uniform, to show how we belong to various groups.

PREPARATION

A collection of headgear is needed: a hat from the uniform of your particular organisation, a helmet from a suit of armour, a crown, and a phylactery (which can be made from a matchbox attached to a headband, painted black). A polystyrene head, as found in shop window displays, could be used, or a volunteer (or four) could be recruited.

PRESENTATION

We can often tell a lot about people from what they wear, and if they have special clothes, there is usually a hat—so we'll concentrate on hats!

(Place uniform hat on display.) What do we know about people who wear hats like this one? They belong to (name of organisation). They don't just wear it to keep heads warm and dry or because it's in fashion—but to show they belong. Look at others who do the same thing: policemen, bishops, etc. Our uniform is a sign that we BELONG to our organisation or group.

(Change to having phylactery on display.) What's this? What do you think might be in the little box? Explain about the command in Deut 6 to wear God's commands on the forehead, and how this was taken literally. What does it say about the wearer? He BELONGS to

God's people, and is instantly recognisable as such—and that he takes God's word seriously, too.

(Now place helmet on display.) Who would have worn one of these? Why? Look at Eph 6 to see what the helmet (and indeed the rest of the armour) is all about. (See also Talk 54 on the Armour of God.) While we don't wear these things today, like the phylactery, they are symbols of BELONGING—this time to God's army. They are also signs that we have taken Paul's advice and 'put on' all that God gives us to enable us to live for him.

(Now the crown.) And these are worn by...? Kings and queens, of course. But this represents another sort of crown we read of—the crown of life (1 Pet 5:4). This shows that we BELONG to heaven, and is promised to all those who have lived for Jesus. That may begin with belonging to (organisation); it will certainly continue with listening to and acting on God's word; and it will go on by acting what God gives us in Paul's list of armour.

Ian J Hutchings
Partington, Manchester

85   A Scout/Guide Is a Friend To Animals

TEXT

Gen 1:25–6; see also Gen 9:1–7; Is 1:3.

AIM

This talk was one of several on the Scout Law given at parade services, with the intention of relating the Scout Law to Bible teaching, and to the Scout's duty to God.

PREPARATION

I deliberately had no visual aid, seeing that most, if not all the congregation had animal pets. I also called upon the congregation's corporate biblical knowledge. However, if you have facilities for showing a filmstrip, preferably using a daylight screen, then there is a beautiful strip, *The Creation*, based on Gen 1–2 that would be well worth showing. (Distributed by Concordia Films, Number NZ-1. See Appendix.)

PRESENTATION

Ask any in the congregation who have Bibles to look up the main text and read it to them. (Or reread it, if it has been included in the service already as part of the Bible reading.)
    Make three main points:

1   *Scouts should respect animals as part of God's creation*
    By questioning, draw out that God created everything very good, that he is concerned for all living creatures, hungry birds, lost sheep, animals that fall into pits, etc. Jesus evidently had masterly control of the donkey colt he used on Palm Sunday.
2   *God has given us dominion over the animal creation*
    Refer again to our opening text and also Gen 9:2. Draw out the

clear distinction between man and animal. Animals were created after their kind, may have self-consciousness, but limited power to reason, and no sense of morality (they cannot sin), being governed chiefly by instinct. God, however, made man as a distinct being in his own image, so we are vastly more important than animals.

Attempt to draw out biblical comparisons, eg, Jesus says we are more valuable than sparrows (Mt 10:31); he allowed 2,000 swine to drown to help save Legion from demonic power (Mk 5:13). Animals may be eaten as food by man (Gen 9:3). Hence draw out that we must not be over-sentimental about animals. They should be kept in their rightful place. We should obviously care for them. However, some people seem to have more concern for animals than for starving, homeless refugees, for example.

3 *We can learn important lessons from the animal creation*
Quote Is 1:3. The animal recognises its master and will usually be faithful, affectionate and loyal to one master. But we frequently do not recognise the one who rightly has dominion over us, not just because he made us (see Ps 95:6 and 100:3), but also because, through his Son, the Lord Jesus, he redeemed us on the cross. This point could be illustrated with the story of the boy who lost the boat he had made, but then saw it in a shop. He had to buy it back before he could say he owned it again; so it was now his, both by creation and redemption.

End with the challenge that if we are exercising our rightful dominion over the animal kingdom, are we allowing the Lord Jesus to exercise his rightful dominion over us?

Michael Botting
Editor

PART FIVE
Wedding Talks

Introduction

'The most important day of their lives'—this is how most people regard their forthcoming wedding; and we who have the responsibility of conducting weddings should aim to make this ideal a reality. Many who seek to be married in church have little knowledge of what a church wedding is all about. Some only choose a church setting so that it will look good in the photographs; others for purely sentimental reasons desire a traditional church setting. Either way, the majority of those who come to be married in church have very little understanding of Christian belief and practice, and so a family-service approach is not out of place.

There are those who question the appropriateness of offering a church wedding for those who have not been baptised and have no interest in Christian things. However, while the present British law stands, it is best to regard the taking of weddings as a special opportunity rather than a necessary duty. A wedding is surely an opportunity to share something helpful concerning the relevance of Christ to their lives. It is worth taking care and trouble over therefore. In a large parish, where there are many weddings every year, there will be few people in the course of ten years who have not attended the church for a wedding or a funeral at some time. It is up to those conducting the service to make it both memorable and enjoyable.

It is good to include in every wedding service a talk that is brief, gripping and meaningful. In this respect it is useful to choose an appropriate verse from the Bible, and write it on a card, preferably with a picture of the church on the cover. You can joke with the bridegroom that he will have no excuse in future years for not remembering the Anniversary, because the date is also written on the card! Here, the place of humour is important. It helps to lessen feelings of tension and awkwardness if the whole congregation is allowed to laugh at some time during the proceedings. Experience indicates that a small and somewhat humorous 'wedding present' makes for memorability! The choice of verse from the Bible is also important: it should have some relevance either to the time of year, or to the interests of the couple concerned. One good illustration can be used again and again, and the talk improves in fluency each time it is given.

Stephen Trapnell
Basingstoke

86 Wedding or Marriage?

'That is why a man leaves his father and mother and is united with his wife, and they become one' (Gen 2:24 GNB).

PRESENTATION

(Explain the context of the verse, and its relevance for marriage today.)

Have you ever thought? What is the difference between a 'wedding' and a 'marriage'? If you look the words up in a dictionary, you will see no distinction is made. But, come to think of it, there is a difference. I wonder, on your invitation, were you invited to a wedding or a marriage? When the wedding is over, the marriage begins. You can buy a wedding, but you can't buy a marriage! A wedding lasts about half an hour (thirty-three minutes and twenty-seven seconds is what I tell people!) but a marriage lasts a lifetime.

I have a small wedding present for you! (Produce a small tube of glue, and describe it for strength and durability.) What happens when one's fingers are stuck with Super Glue? God is like glue! He for his part makes a perfect bond that never comes unstuck. Stick to him, and stick with one another, and you will find that he will stick close to you. He can make a marriage out of a wedding.

Stephen Trapnell
Basingstoke

87   The Lord Is Your Keeper

The Lord is your Keeper....

The Lord will keep you from all evil;
he will keep your life.

The Lord will keep your going out
and your coming in
from this time forth and for evermore
(Ps 121:5, 7–8 RSV).

PRESENTATION

Here is a glorious promise for you both. It speaks of the Lord as your
Keeper. It does not mean a keeper as at the zoo, where you would
feel encaged and have no freedom. Rather, it is one who looks after
you, and guards and guides your life. He will keep your coming and
going—all the way through the new life that you start together
today. It is God's promise to you!

I have a very simple wedding present for you by way of illustration.
(Produce a large bolt with two nuts on it.) Marriage in some ways
resembles a nut and bolt: in engineering terms, we even speak of male
and female threads. They are made for each other. Here, though, there
is a second nut, and this is called a 'keeper nut'. Screwed against the
other nut tightly, it prevents the union from working loose. No
matter how much buffeting, the nut and bolt never separate.

In Christian marriage, Christ is like the keeper nut. The closer
you are bonded to him, the stronger is your bond to one another.
'The Lord himself is your Keeper!' (I bet you have never been called
a nut in church before!) Give Christ a place in your future life
together. He will look after you. He will guard you and guide you.
He will keep you.

Stephen Trapnell
Basingstoke

266

88 'Get Plastered!'
(Especially suitable for Ascensiontide weddings)

TEXT
Jesus said, 'I am with you always' (Mt 28:20 RSV).

PRESENTATION

An easy text to find, and an easy one to remember! Just five words!
It is a promise—a promise of Jesus to his disciples, before he left
them and went back to heaven. It is a promise which is also true for
us today. Countless people all down the ages have found the truth of
this text, and have been encouraged as a result. Today, Christ says
to you: 'I am with you always!'

Christ promises to stand by you both. He will never leave you on
your own, nor let you down. He will be with you in good times and
bad. He will stick to you!

I have a wedding present for you—something very inexpensive.
Something to help you remember this promise of Jesus. (Reveal a
piece of Elastoplast.) This is the plaster that sticks to you through
thick and thin. It says, 'For cushioned protection'—I find that a
little cushioned protection goes a long way. Christ is like this plaster.
He sticks to you. He covers all your hurts. He heals your sores. He is
with you always!

One final word. Don't you dare go out from this church and say
the minister told you to go and get plastered!

Stephen Trapnell
Basingstoke

89 Wedding Harmony
(Especially suitable for those with musical interests)

'May the God of steadfastness and encouragement grant you to live in such harmony with one another, in accord with Christ Jesus, that together you may with one voice glorify the God and Father of our Lord Jesus Christ' (Rom 15:5–6 RSV).

PRESENTATION

This verse is written in the form of a prayer; it could be a prayer for you today. It speaks about God, and it speaks about us.

It says that God is one who is steadfast and encouraging. He does not change. He gives endurance and encouragement to us. It is the quality of 'stickability' that is spoken of here—something that we all of us need. So we have hope for the days ahead.

This verse also prays for us. It speaks of a two-sided bond or union. 'Grant you to live in such harmony with one another, [that's one side] in accord with Christ Jesus, [that's the other side] that together you may with one voice glorify the God and Father of our Lord Jesus Christ.' Notice the mention of 'harmony' and 'one voice'.

What is the difference between 'harmony' and 'unison'? Unison is when you sing the same tune, and so make music; many people think of marriage as like that. But unison, though often glorious, is sometimes dull; it is harmony that makes the music exciting and interesting. Christian marriage can also be like singing in harmony, in which each plays his or her own part in time with the other, and though the parts are different, they blend to make harmony and music.

May you glorify the Lord Jesus Christ in the music of marriage that you make together!

Stephen Trapnell
Basingstoke

90 Two into One Won't Go

Text

'For He is our peace, who has made us both one' (Eph 2:14 RSV).

Presentation

I never could do arithmetic. However, I remember being told at school that, 'Two into one won't go.' Here I am now, some thirty or forty years later, in every wedding service proving that, 'Two into one will go!' In Christian marriage, this happens all the time, and God is the one who makes it possible.

Explain that the text refers to Jew and Gentile, who had no love for one another. Humanly speaking, it was an impossible mix, but God still made them one. If this is what God can do for those opposed to one another, think what he can do for those who love one another!

The whole service is a picture of two becoming one. (Hence the joining of hands and the giving and receiving of rings.) Have you ever thought how a wedding-ring is made? It is not a fraction of an inch cut off a gold pipe, smoothed and polished up. Rather, it is a gold bar, with the ends bent round and joined together so that one can't see where they have been joined. A wedding-ring is therefore not just a sign of being married, but it is a picture of marriage itself. Two becoming one, and Christ is the one who makes this possible.

(This talk can be illustrated by having two lighted candles, which the couple hold during the explanation, and then together they light a third candle. The first two candles are then extinguished, and their new life together is pictured for all to see as the third candle is held high.)

Stephen Trapnell
Basingstoke

Appendix

BOOKS, AUDIO-VISUAL AIDS AND EQUIPMENT

Books

All Age Worship, Maggie Durran, (Angel Press).

All Generations, The Offchurch Group, (CIO): a handbook for leaders of family worship.

All Assembly Services, R. H. Lloyd, (The Religious Education Press).

Angels with Dirty Faces, Ishmael, (Kingsway).

Children in the Way: A Report from the General Synod Board of Education (NS/Church House Publishing).

Children of the Voice, Ishmael, (Kingsway).

Church Family Worship, Michael Perry (ed), (Hodder & Stoughton).

Church Family Worship Resources Book (Church Pastoral Aid Society).

Family Services, Kenneth Stevenson, (Alcuin Club Manual No.3/SPCK).

For All the Family, Michael Botting (ed), (Kingsway).

The Gateways of The Stars, George H. Morrison, (Hodder & Stoughton).

The Good Wine, Josephine Bax, (Church House Publishing).

Help, I Can't Draw!, Sheila Pigrem (Kingsway).

Help! There's a Child in My Church, Peter Graystone, (Scripture Union).

'Home to Home: Towards a Biblical Model of the Family', *Anvil*, vol 3, no 3 (1986), Michael Moynagh.

Know How to Encourage Family Worship, H. Mellor, (Scripture Union).

Know How—Special Events for All the Family, S. H. Clark, (Scripture Union).

Making Contact, Leslie Francis, (Collins).

Patterns for Worship: A Report by the Liturgical Commission of the Church of England (Church House Publishing).

The Sacrament of the Word, Donald Coggan, (Collins).

Something to Say to the Children, John Gray, (T & T Clark).

Sunday Learning for All Ages, Judith Rose, (Grove Booklets, Pastoral Series 11).

Today's Children, Tomorrow's Church, Margaret Old, (Scripture Union).

UK Christian Handbook, Peter Brierley (ed), (MARC Europe). Lists sources of educational supplies, art supplies, audio-visual services, audio libraries, film-hire libraries, etc—a generally indispensable source of information, indexed by organisational name, location and personnel.

Teaching the Families, Michael Botting, (Falcon).

To Teach Others Also, R. Hudson Pope, (Scripture Union).

Using the Bible with All Ages Together, D. L. and P. R. Griggs, (Bible Society).

Using the Bible with Audio-Visuals, D. L. Griggs, (Bible Society).

Women and Children First: Exploring the Christian Meaning of Family. This was the theme of the 1987 Anglican Evangelical Assembly. Full scripts of the papers can be obtained from the Secretary, 43 Bristol Road, Chippenham, Wilts, SN15 1NT.

Drama

Back to Back's Little Black Paperback Book, Fraser Grace, (Kingsway).

The Drama Recipe Book, MacDonald and Stickley, (Minstrel).

The Greatest Burger Ever Sold, Nick McIvor, (Minstrel).

Know How to use Drama in Church, Gillian Grinham, (Scripture Union).

Laughter in Heaven, Murray Watts, (MARC).

Lightning Sketches, Paul Burbridge and Murray Watts, (Hodder & Stoughton).

Mime: The Next Step, Geoffrey Stevenson, (Minstrel).

Move Yourselves, Gordon and Ronnie Lamont, (Scripture Union).

One Stage Further, Nigel Forde, (MARC).

Playing with Fire, Paul Burbridge, (MARC).

Red Letter Days, Paul Burbridge and Murray Watts, (Hodder & Stoughton).

Scene One, Ashley Martin, Andy Kelso et al, (Kingsway).

Steps of Faith, Geoffrey and Judith Stevenson, (Kingsway).

Theatrecraft, Nigel Forde, (MARC).

Time to Act, Paul Burbridge and Murray Watts, (Hodder & Stoughton).

Using the Bible in Drama, Stickley and Belben, (Bible Society).

Equipment

Daylight translucent screen material for back-projection of film-strips or OHP transparencies can be obtained from Triumph Communications Ltd, Nathanael House, 21–23 High Street, Bassingham, Lincs LN5 9JZ (0522 858115), who also supply a wide range of audio-visual material. Write for catalogue.

Magiboards Ltd, Stafford Park 12, Telford, Shropshire TF3 3BJ (0952 292111) provide a wide range of visual-aid boards and accompanying materials.

'Teazlegraph' was originally marketed under this name by E. J. Arnold & Sons of Leeds, but is no longer supplied by this company. A similar result can be obtained by purchasing *nylon* velvet from any good quality fabric supplier and gluing it on to a sheet of plywood, say 5′ x 4′ (1.6 x 1.3 m), with a dowel frame added. This should be erected on an easel. In order to attach anything to this board, stick Velcro discs about ¼″ or 1cm square on to the back of the object concerned, the number of discs depending on its size, using a strong glue like Evostik or Uhu. When the Velcro comes into contact with the nylon velvet, it will adhere so well that it can even be used out of doors when there is a wind. Velcro can be obtained from a good haberdashers.

Overhead projector aids

Bible Map Transparencies (Abingdon) available from Lion Publishing, Peter's Way, Sandy Lane West, Littlemore, Oxford, OX4 5HG

(0865 747550) or from Scripture Union (see Audio Visual Aids, page 275).

Computer desktop transparencies for OHPs can be made for those who have access to a Hewlet Packard graphics plotter, model 7550A with Logos Graphics, 23 Nottingham Road, Stapleford, Nottingham NG9 8AB (0602 391711). This firm claims to offer the best prices in the country for top quality British machines, accessories, etc.

Help, I can't draw!, four pictorial workbooks of the Bible by Sheila Pigrem (see booklist above).

Know How to Use an Overhead Projector (Scripture Union), S. H. Clark.

Lotus Free-lance Plus software for use on IBM, Amstrad, etc. Clergy may find members of their congregation in industry who have such equipment available.

Picture it! (Bible Society), Paul Clowney.

Transart Visual Products, Transart Group Ltd, Courtyard Communications Ltd, Farm Hall Office, West Street, Godmanchester, Huntingdon, Cambs (tel: 0480 411143; fax: 0480 455252; telex: 32170) produce a wide range of OHP transparencies. Write for catalogue.

Note: Colour photographs on good quality paper (art paper or paper with chalky surface is best) can be lifted from magazines in the following way, provided copyright permission has first been obtained:

1 Remove the picture from the magazine and cover with sticky-back book-film, sticky side down on picture, making sure that bubbles do *not* occur.
2 Place the whole in a bowl of water to soak off the backing paper. The ink of the picture will be left on the 'tacky back'.

3   When dry, cover this with an acetate and you have a lovely full-colour picture for your OHP. You can add titles, or whatever, with your ordinary OHP pens.

Audio-visual aids

Filmstrips and videos can be obtained from quite a number of sources:

Bible Society, Stonehill Green, Westlea, Swindon SN5 7DG (0793 513713).

Church Army Resource Centre, Independence Road, London SE3 9LG (081-318 1226).

Church Pastoral Aid Society, Athena Drive, Tachbrook Park, Warwick, CV34 6NG (0926 334242).

Concordia Publishing House, 28 Huntingdon Road, Cambridge CB3 0HH (0223 65113).

Scripture Union [for hire of videos and soundstrips], 9–11 Clothier Road, Brislington, Bristol BS4 5RL (0272 771131); [for purchase of videos, soundstrips and sound cassettes] PO Box 38, Bristol BS99 7NA. The material mentioned in Talks 63 to 68 can be obtained from here. Write for catalogue.

SPCK, Holy Trinity Church, Marylebone Road, London NW1 (071-387 5282).

Other material especially recommended for selective use at family services:

Bible News Ltd, Holland House, 39–40 Hythe Road, London NW10 6UN, publish on cassettes news broadcasts of biblical events in the idiom of modern-news reporting. There are five cassettes covering ten programmes in each series: *Abraham to King Saul* and *The Jesus Programme*. (Part of the broadcast on Goliath is recommended in Talk 65.)

The Dramatised Bible published by the Bible Society and Marshall Pickering and edited by Michael Perry is particularly recommended by CPAS for use in family services.

Other useful sources of information

Administry, 69 Sandridge Road, St Albans, Herts AL1 4AG (0727 56370), include occasional papers on family services.

Boys' Brigade, 1 Kings Terrace, Galena Road, Hammersmith, London W6 0LT (081-741 4001).

CARE (Christian action and research organisation) publishes a free magazine, *Care for the Family*. Information from 53 Romney Street, London SW1P 3RF (071-233 0455).

Familybase, Jubilee House, 3 Hooper Street, Cambridge CB1 2NZ (0223 311596), initiator of the Family Charter concerned to help strengthen family life in the United Kingdom.

Learning All Together, published quarterly by Scripture Union, 130 City Road, London EC1V 2NJ (071-782 0013), providing weekly material for all ages, both for worship and Bible study.

Look Hear! A magazine published termly that incorporates *Media Review* and *AVA Magazine*. Subscriptions Secretary, 1 Briarswood, Springfield, Chelmsford, Essex CM1 5UH.

Maintenance & Equipment News, published quarterly by Crown Wood Publications Ltd, PO Box 249, Ascot, Berks SL5 0BZ (0344 59528), and sent free of charge to all Anglican clergy, frequently contains AVA information.

Music copyright: for information contact Christian Music Association, Glyndley Manor, Stone Cross, East Sussex BN24 5BS (0323 841419), which also publishes a quarterly magazine entitled *Worship*.

Book copyright: see the reverse of the title-page (in almost every book) for information about what is or is not reproducible—by any means. When in doubt, write to the Permissions Department of the relevant publisher. Explain precisely:

1   What passage or artwork you wish to use

2 How it will be reproduced
3 The intended circulation of the material
4 Whether there is any charge involved for viewers/recipients.

You should ask for the proper acknowledgement wording.

Biblical Index

C = Crossword talk, P = Parade-service talk, W = Wedding talk

Subject Index

(Wedding talks not included)

CPAS 'Church Leadership Pack'

If you have found this book useful, you may be interested to know that similar talks are available on a regular basis through a CPAS mailing called 'Church Leadership Pack'. Published three times a year, 'Church Leadership Pack' includes up to 50 sides of A4 in loose-leaf format for filing and provides practical, usable material for ministers and churches, for example: courses to photocopy or adapt, quotes to enliven sermons, up-to-date lists of audio-visual and other resources, briefings on a range of ministry situations to stimulate and inform, projects for the church, plus family service ideas. These include ideas on worship, teaching and music, all-age talks, and sermon ideas—often with OHP masters.

'Church Leadership Pack' is available on subscription only, from the Adult Training and Resources Unit, CPAS, Athena Drive, Tachbrook Park, Warwick CV34 6NG (0926 334242) at around £12 per year (three issues).

For All The Family

by Michael Botting

First published in 1984 and reprinted many times by popular demand, *For All The Family* brings together 80 outline talks for all seasons—many illustrated—to help ministers and family service speakers to ensure that their message is biblical, clear and memorable.

'This splendidly practical book will be of great help to those teaching in the context of the family. Biblical themes are presented in lively fashion with copious use of visual aids and overhead projector. The result is an attractive range of lessons which ought to capture the interest of adults and youngsters alike.'

From the Foreword by the Bishop of Ripon

Kingsway Publications

Angels With Dirty Faces

by Ishmael

Ishmael loves children. Here's how—and why.

'Through all the years I've never known anyone who can so motivate children in worship, or lead them so securely into the things of the Spirit of God.'
—Jim Graham, Pastor,
Goldhill Baptist Church.

Kingsway Publications